AFN
AUSTRALIAN FISHING NETWORK

LET'S START FISHING

BILL CLASSON • ANDY HAHN

Photography: Bill Classon, Morgue File, Andy Hahn

US Book Shop Distributors
Cardinal Publishers Group
2222 Hillside Avenue
Suite 100
Indianapolis, IN 46218
Tel: (317) 879 0871
Fax: (317) 879 0872
    (317) 846 1557
Toll free: (800) 296 0481
Email: info@cardinalpub.com
Web: www.cardinalpub.com

First published in 2007
Australian Fishing Network
1/48 Centre Way
South Croydon VIC 3136
Australia
Tel: (03) 9761 4044
Fax: (03) 9761 4055
Email: sales@afn.com.au
Website: afn.com.au

Copyright © AFN 2007
Designed by Joy Eckermann

ISBN No. 9781 8651 3115 3

CONTENTS

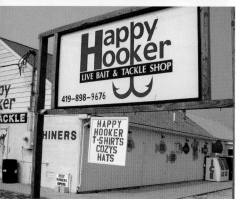

INTRODUCTION

Welcome to fishing and the fun, challenges and excitement that go with one of the world's most popular pastimes. Fishing can take you to some great places in our magnificent country while filling your eyes with scenery and action that others almost never see. It offers opportunities to learn about nature, water, animals, birds, fish and most important of all, yourself.

Going fishing can mean walking a mountain stream, paddling a canoe, riding on a boat, watching the sun come up on a misty lake or just enjoying the company of friends down on the local pier.

This book aims to provide enough information to get you started in whichever type of angling you'd like to try. It explains the different types of fishing you can do, discusses the tackle you need and why you need it, how to use it, how to hook and land or release fish, and how to look after the environment so it will assure healthy recreation for your children in the future.

When pursued with passion, fishing is a tremendous and fulfilling sport, and one that you will enjoy for your whole life— and that's something to look forward to!

For most of the fishing you'll do in this modern age, you'll need some hooks (and probably sinkers and other bits and pieces of what's called "terminal tackle"), some line, a reel to store your line on, and a rod to help you cast out and then control and bring in a hooked fish. It's also handy to have a tackle box, a bucket for your bait and your catch, and maybe a knife to trim line, cut up bait and clean the fish you want to eat... And that's about it! Later, as you learn more about fishing and get more involved in the sport, you might want to add items to your tackle collection, but what I've just described will get you off to a flying start. So, let's have a look at this gear.

CHAPTER 1
TACKLE

HANDLINES

Despite advances in fishing tackle technology the humble handline is still a great way to catch fish. Handlines are easy to carry, cost very little and catch lots of fish. They are also very sensitive and transmit every touch or bite back to the angler's index finger.

When buying handlines, just match the size of the line to the fish being sought. A light 7–10 lb handline is best for small fish up to 1 lb, 8–14 lb lines are good for fish up to about 3 lb and then you need to go heavier if you're after larger, predatory fish.

Handlines are often sold ready rigged at many tackle shops. These lines are wrapped on a cork or on a plastic spool known as a handcaster. The plastic spool can be used to store line neatly to make casting easier.

To cast with this gear, the handspool is gripped on the inside of the spool and the spool is held open faced in the desired casting direction. The other hand throws the weighted sinker using a couple of helicopter type rotations before release. With a little practice, quite good casts can be made.

The fish is hooked by holding the line between the thumb and forefinger and pulling your arm back towards your chest. Once hooked retrieve the line hand over hand laying the line in neat coils.

If the fish is large enough to stress or break the line as it fights, ease the pressure between thumb and

CATFISH WHISKERS
Catfish often go on the prowl at night and have no problem finding something to eat in dark or muddy water. Their whiskers, also called barbels, contain highly specialized nerve cells that detect odors. So catfish use their whiskers like a nose to sniff out food!

For this reason, "stink baits" such as cheese, chicken liver and scented doughballs work well for catfish.

forefinger and let some line out. This is the most basic and sensitive drag system ever developed and good training for all anglers.

For anyone who wants to enjoy their fishing without paying too much money, a couple of handlines provide an excellent starting point.

HINT BOX

How much line to put on a handcaster

All handcasters should be filled so that the line sits to at least half the depth of the spool. On deep spooled models, where such a large line capacity is not required, you can raise the line level by using a material such as string or even old line as backing. This is put on before the main line to build up the spool.

As a final point, when filling a handcaster or cork with fresh line, always remember to apply sufficient tension so that it packs down tightly and doesn't spring off the spool.

REELS

A fishing reel serves as a tool for storing, casting and retrieving line, although some, like fly reels, are not designed to help with casting. Every fishing reel has a spool of some sort to store line on, a handle that turns to bring in line, and a foot for mounting to a rod. Most modern reels also have a drag, which allows line to be pulled from the reel's spool under a pre-set tension when a big fish is hooked, preventing the line from breaking.

Fact Box

TYPE OF REEL—CLOSED FACE

Push-button control makes closed-face (also called spincast) reels quite easy to cast. They are a good choice for young fishermen because the cover protects the spool and prevents the line from tangling. These inexpensive reels are often sold as "combos" with matching rods and fit the bill perfectly for freshwater species such as bluegill, perch and catfish.

Fact Box

TYPE OF REEL—BAITRUNNER

Baitrunners are an adaption built onto spinning reels to enable fish to take a bait and move off under very light but controlled drag. This function is engaged by a lever at the back of the reel body.

Baitrunner reels are designed for catching large freshwater catfish and saltwater fish such as sailfish and dolphin because these species need to be given line and time to swallow the bait after they take it.

A turn of the handle puts the reel into normal fishing mode to hook and fight the fish.

Fact Box

TYPE OF REEL—SPINNING

Spinning reels are the most popular kind for anglers of all ages because they are versatile, easy to use and very functional. Their simplicity and ease of use makes them perfect for young anglers who are ready to step up from a closed-face reel.

Spinning reels get their name from the spinning, outer rotor on the reel, which revolves around a fixed spool. The line is laid neatly onto the spool as an oscillating gear moves the spool back and forth during the retrieve.

Spinning reels all have a drag system that allows you to play fish under the controlled tension set by the drag. They are also geared so that for every turn of the handle, the rotor or head of the reel turns four, five or more times around the spool, depending on the gear ratio. This helps you retrieve line quickly.

Fishermen should keep these reels fully loaded with line to achieve good casting distance. Light lines are also needed to maintain the right balance between casting distance and fish-handling ability.

Most small reels work best with 4- to 8-pound-test lines, medium reels need 8- to 12-pound lines and large reels use 12- to 25-pound line.

Filling the spool

When putting new line on your reel, always hold the line with finger-grip pressure as it feeds off the filler spool in a straight line. Do not allow the line to run off the side of the filler spool because this causes line twist.

Fill the reel to the point where the lip of the spool starts to bend outwards (See Diagram). A little extra line is OK but when you stop, the line should not jump off the spool. If it does, you have overfilled the reel. An

Fact Box

TYPE OF REEL—MOOCHING REEL

Single-action mooching reels feature a 1:1 gear ratio and don't cast well. They are very popular among salmon trollers in British Columbia and Alaska. Anglers typically use these reels with 9-foot or longer rods because they help maintain a tight line during the fight.

Correct line load for spinning reels

Under filled line load for spinning reels

Over filled line load for spinning reels

over full reel will be hard to manage because line tends to flow off the spool and tangle just as you go to cast.

Revolving-spool reels also need to be correctly filled with line in order to work properly. Low amounts of line on revolving-spool reels increase drag pressures, reduce casting distance and limit the retrieve rate.

Fact Box

TYPE OF REEL—FLY REEL

Fly reels are not used for casting. (See Fly Fishing Chapter XXX) Freshwater models are rarely used to fight fish as anglers bring in line by hand; however, saltwater fly reels have strong drag systems for playing large fish.

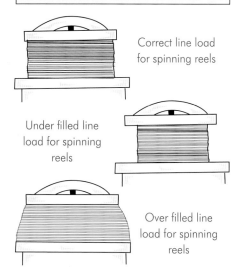

The amount of line on any reel will eventually start to go down with break-offs and wear and tear. In most fishing situations it will not be necessary to refill the whole reel. Just peel back the top 100 yards and add a top shot to fill the spool.

Remember, don't fish with any reel that does not have the correct line load.

Fact Box

TYPE OF REEL— REVOLVING SPOOL

Revolving-spool reels include all sizes from little baitcasters to big-game reels. Learning to cast them takes time and patience.

The trick is to match the rate at which the line leaves the spool with the flight of the lure or bait during the cast. This is done mechanically by adjusting the spool tension or cast control system and combining it with subtle pressure from the thumb during casting.

Casting well with these reels requires lots of practice. Once the reel is correctly adjusted and your thumb becomes "educated," good casting follows naturally.

Small baitcasters are mostly used for casting and trolling lures in fresh water and shallow salt water. They do not cast into the wind as well as spinning reels but they are very accurate at short range. These smaller reels are often fished on pistol-grip type rods that provide a comfortable hand fit to the rod/reel combination.

Larger baitcasters and surf reels are fished on two-handed rods to gain maximum casting power and distance. They are used on boats and by shorebound anglers. Carefully consider gear ratios when deciding which of these reels to use. High-speed ratios of 5:1 or 6:1 perform best with lures while ratios of 4:1 or 5:1 get the call for more general work. These reels work best from medium- and fast-taper rods.

HINT BOX

Caring for your drag

Drags need to be free of dirt and debris to work properly, so cleaning them at least once a year with kerosene or a degreaser is a good idea. Most drags are coated with a light grease to protect the washers; make sure you re-grease the washers when you put the drag back together. If unsure how to do this, your local tackle shop can help you.

Drags also rely on having flat surfaces to run on. Always loosen the drag tension when you put a reel away. If you put it away with a tightened drag system, the washers may "set" or warp into that shape. This will make the drag rough and jerky, causing lost fish or lost enjoyment if the equipment does not perform properly.

Setting a drag

Drag systems are provided on most reels to allow the angler to fight fish with a preset and controlled amount of tension. The aim of the drag is to pay out line when the pull of the fish exceeds the amount of tension set on the drag. Many anglers have trouble adjusting their drag so that it both sets the hook and fights fish correctly.

Generally, the drag should be set so that it is firm but not so tight that it will break the line. The line should slip off the reel but under controlled pressure. You can check this by tying the line to a fixed object, like a fence,

did you know ...

GEAR RATIO

The gear ratio of a fishing reel refers to the number of times the spool rotates per turn of the handle.

For example, when one turn of the handle causes the spool to rotate three times, the reel has a gear ratio of 3 to 1 (usually written as 3:1).

Most fishermen consider 3:1 as a low gear ratio while 6:1 ranks as a high ratio.

Low-ratio (also called low-speed) reels are used when plenty of winding power is needed, as in deep-sea bottom fishing. High-speed reels prove most useful when targeting fast-feeding fish with lures, or anywhere a fast retrieve is required to make the lure attractive to the fish.

and then pulling with the rod and reel. The rod should curve to a firm, solid arc before the line starts slipping off the reel.

The whole purpose of the drag is to provide this slipping mechanism so the line does not break under pressure from fish. It lets fish run but keeps you in control.

It takes a little experimentation to get it right. If the drag slips when you simply lift the rod or try to wind in line, then it's set too lightly. If you break off when you hook a fish, it is set too tightly. Always take time to set the drag correctly each time you fish. Getting the drag setting right is an essential part of catching quality fish.

RODS

A fishing rod is basically a stick. To be more precise, it's a flexible shaft, usually fitted with guides to carry the fishing line, and a place to mount a reel.

Fishing rods allow you to cast your bait beyond bank-side obstructions like bushes and rocks, and they keep your line off the side of a boat or away from barnacle-encrusted jetty pylons. Rods also make very useful bite indicators and shock absorbers when hooking, playing and landing fish.

The rod must suit the type of fishing you plan to do, but with so many models on the market it's often difficult to select one that meets your needs. The best rod depends on where you fish and what you are fishing for; you may need several rod and reel combinations to get the most from your fishing.

When comparing and choosing rods, take into account these important points.

Taper

A rod's taper describes the rate at which the blank narrows from its relatively thick butt to its thin tip. Most of the rods displayed in shops today are built on hollow, tubular shafts (called blanks) made of fiberglass or a mixture of graphite and fiberglass. They are light, fairly strong and fun to use, but

did you know ...

TELESCOPIC ROD

A telescopic rod, as the name implies, features sections that slide up inside each other for ease of storage and transport.

While telescopic rods where once seen as gimmicks, rod manufacturers today make very good models that are ideal for anyone who uses public transportation or has limited carrying space. Telescopic rods fit in a backpack, briefcase, bike bag or suitcase and can mean the difference between going fishing and missing out.

Maintenance is especially important with telescopic rods, and they should always be washed and wiped clean of grit and sand before being collapsed. Always store telescopic rods in their collapsed or unextended shape. This prevents joints from seizing or sticking together.

you do need to be a bit careful with them because they're certainly not unbreakable!

The shape of the blank determines the rod's taper, and the amount of fiberglass or graphite in the rod determines its weight.

Slow-tapered rods are generally used for live-bait fishing and provide a soft, uniform curve suited to handling small- to medium-sized fish.

Medium-taper rods are very good for bait fishing. They can cast lighter weights, have a softer delivery and act as a good shock absorber when fighting strong fish.

Use fast-taper rods when casting distance is needed, particularly with lures. Fast-taper rods also put more pressure or leverage on fish during the fight.

It's also important to match tip action and sensitivity to the type of fishing you do. Finer, light-tipped rods tend to provide better casting action and more sensitivity for detecting bites compared to heavy-tipped rods.

Reel Seats

The reel attaches to the rod at the reel seat. Different types of rods have reel seats in distinct locations on a rod. Fly reels mount low on the rod, near the end of the butt; spinning reels attach at the handle's midsection and baitcasting reels sit fairly far up the handle. Each mount is situated to provide the most energy-efficient casting position for each type of reel.

Hands

You may have to use one or both hands when casting with different kinds of fishing rods.

Most light spinning reels and baitcasters are

worked on one-handed rods.
Only one hand is used in the casting process. This type of rod is most commonly used for freshwater and light-tackle saltwater fishing.

Larger spinning reels, baitcasters and medium-sized revolving-spool reels work best on two-handed rods. Both hands are used in the casting process.

Two-handed rods usually allow the angler to generate more power on the cast, providing greater distance with the appropriate tackle. Two-handed rods also help when fighting tough fish for any length of time. They allow the angler to transfer the weight of the fish into a rod belt rather than absorbing it through his wrists. Two-handed rods are used in blue-water and surfcasting situations.

HINT BOX

Circle Hooks

Because of their odd shape, circle hooks look like they would never hold a fish. Don't be fooled! Circle hooks are very effective in latching on to a fish's jaw rather than lodging in the gut or gullet, making them a good choice for fishermen who practice catch and release. Setting the hook requires a special technique: Rather than briskly lifting the rod, point the rod tip at the fish and crank the reel steadily to imbed the hook.

HOOKS

Don't worry too much about the different hook shapes or patterns. They all work, and you won't really need to choose specialized patterns when you're just getting started. Getting the hook's size right is far more important. As I like to say, you can catch a big fish on a small hook, but it's much harder to catch a small fish on a big hook! So, if in doubt, choose a smaller hook rather than a bigger one.

The numbering code used for hook sizing is really rather complicated. There's no easy way to explain this next bit, so pay attention while we do our best, because you'll need to come to terms with hook sizing at some stage.

Hooks range from tiny little things intended to catch tiddlers, right up to giant contraptions that look capable of holding an ocean-going ship. Their different sizes are described by a number, and this number refers to the width of the gape or gap (the distance between the point and the shank) rather than the overall length of the hook.

The really confusing part is the fact that the smallest hooks are described by the biggest numbers (I told you it was complicated!). So, a No. 24 hook isn't much bigger

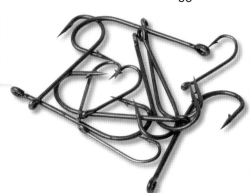

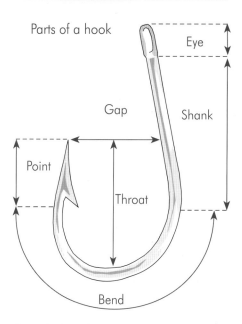

Parts of a hook

Eye

Gap

Shank

Point

Throat

Bend

than the head of a pin, while a No. 12 hook is just about perfect for catching sunfish and trout. A No. 2 is significantly larger again, and is a very good size for targeting catfish and bait.

This sizing system, with the hook gape or width increasing as the number describing it decreases, continues until we hit No. 1. A No. 1 hook is a very useful, all-round size for many kinds of fish, from porgies and pompano in saltwater to bigger catfish in fresh water. But there are a lot of larger hook sizes than a No. 1. Strangely, these bigger hooks are described by an ascending

ANCIENT AND HISTORICAL FISH HOOKS

The fish hook is one of mankind's oldest tools. The earliest fish hooks were straight, not curved like they are today. They were made from lengths of bone, stone, shell or deer antler sharpened to a very fine point at each end. The line was tied around a groove in the hook's middle.

This "hook" was embedded length-wise in a piece of bait and after it was swallowed, a pull on the line would cause the pointed shaft to cross and stick in the fish's gut.

Later, hooks started to take on the characteristic curve we associate with modern day hooks although many were still made of the same materials as the original hooks.

(increasing) series of numbers, followed by a slash and a zero. Thus, the next size up from a No. 1 is a 1/0, then comes a 3/0, a 4/0 and so on. The very biggest hooks—intended for catching sharks, marlin and giant tuna—are in the 18/0 to 20/0 range, and would look right at home hanging from a crane on a comstruction site!

Most of the fishing you are likely to do when getting started will be well covered by the hook sizes between No. 12 and about 6/0. Hooks smaller than No. 12 are mainly of interest to fly-fishers making imitations of tiny insects to fool trout, while sizes larger than 6/0 are for people going way offshore to chase really big fish.

As the actual variation in size between each hook number is pretty small, sizes can easily be skipped when you're putting together a basic collection of hooks. So, all you really need are some No.12, 10, 8, 6, 4, 1, 2/0, 4/0 and maybe 6/0 hooks… That's plenty! In fact, if you intend to fish only in freshwater or shallow salt water, you can skip the 2/0s, 4/0s and 6/0s.

Fact Box

FISH SPECIES AND HOOKS

Species	Size	Type
FRESHWATER		
Bass (Largemouth and Smallmouth)	4–1/0	Baitholder/Kahle
Catfish (up to 5 pounds)	4–1	Baitholder/Circle
Catfish (over 5 pounds)	1/0–4/0	Baitholder/Circle
Carp	6–2	Baitholder
Northern Pike	1–4/0	O'Shaughnessy/Kahle
Perch	10–6	Baitholder
Salmon	4–1	Baitholder
Sucker	8–6	Baitholder
Sunfish (Bluegill, Crappie)	12–6	Baitholder/Aberdeen
Trout	8–6	Baitholder
Walleye	4–1	Baitholder/O'Shaughnessy
SALT WATER		
Bluefish	2/0–4/0	O'Shaughnessy
Flounder	2–1/0	Baitholder/O'Shaughnessy
Grouper	2/0–6/0	Live Bait/Octopus
Pompano	6–2	O'Shaughnessy/Kahle
Red Drum	1–4/0	O'Shaughnessy/Octopus
Snook	1–4/0	O'Shaughnessy/Octopus
Spanish Mackerel	1/0–2/0	O'Shaughnessy/Octopus
Speckled Seatrout	1–2/0	O'Shaughnessy
Striped Bass	1/0–4/0	Live Bait/Octopus

Various hook styles

SINKERS

Sinkers add weight to make casting easier and/or to make baits sink. They are usually made of lead and the choice of sinker weight and design depends on where you fish, the water and weather conditions, and the type of fish you are after. While there are many different styles and sizes, most anglers only need two or three types of sinkers and perhaps two or three different sizes of each type.

In most cases, you only need enough sinker weight to make casting relatively easy without anchoring the bait rigidly to the bottom.

The golden rule with sinkers is to use just enough lead to do the job. Many fish will reject a bait because they are suspicious of the weight attached to the line.

Besides taking a bait all the way to the bottom, lead can be used to weight the line so it just sinks slowly for mid-water fish. Usually small split shot are used for this purpose.

To use sinkers properly you need to know a little bit about the main types available and how they work for you.

Types of sinkers

Ball Sinkers
The ball sinker as its name suggests, is just a ball of lead with a hole through the middle for the line. Ball sinkers cast very well and are used for shore fishing, surf casting and general fishing off jetties.

Egg and slip sinkers
These sinkers are all variations on one theme and they are used in most types of fishing. They are particularly useful in strong currents because of their reduced water resistance and low snagging qualities. These sinkers are the best choice for drift fishing rigs and general estuary bottom fishing.

Split shot
These small, ball-shaped sinkers have a cut half way through them rather than a central hole. They are crimped or squeezed closed on the line using pliers. Once closed firmly they stay in place on the line.

Split shot are used to fine-tune the balance on a bobber and when just a tiny amount of lead is required above the bait. Split shot come in handy to add casting weight to light baits when fishing in streams and ponds.

One thing to watch for when using split shot is not to apply too much pressure when crimping them onto the line. If too much pressure is used it can damage the line, so take care.

Bank sinkers
These tapered sinkers with an eye at the thinner end are favored by deep sea anglers in their larger sizes (4 ounces to 2 pounds) and by freshwater fishermen in the smaller sizes (1 to 3 ounces). The bank sinker's shape makes it cast straight when shore fishing or fall quickly to the bottom when fishing from a boat.

Dipsey or teardrop sinkers

These sinkers have a teardrop shape with a barrel swivel molded into the top. These sinkers are great for casting distance and for use with bottomfishing rigs having dropper lines. The swivel helps avoid line twist.

Bullet weights
Shaped like bullets and made of lead, steel or brass, these specialized weights are used in plastic-worm rigs for largemouth bass.

FISH FACT

STARFISH—ECHINODERMS

Starfish, as their name suggests are generally shaped like a star and look slow moving and inoffensive. While some starfish are grazers others are ruthless hunters and move about quite a bit in search of their prey.

Their main prey is molluscs, shellfish of various types. They either tear them open with their powerful arms or just absorb them into their open stomach where all of their legs meet on their underside.

The starfish can actually project its stomach over its prey and eat it outside its body—sounds gruesome. So when you see a cute, little starfish just remember, they are hunters too.

SWIVELS

Swivels are used to minimize twist in your fishing line. They allow the fish, bait or lure to spin or twirl without twisting the line.

They also serve as very convenient attachment points when making

Ball bearing swivel   Barrel swivel   Crane swivel   Rolling swivel

Various swivel styles

HINT BOX

Stop line twist

Line twist can be a constant problem particularly for inexperienced anglers. Fishing lines don't start with any twist its just that anglers do things that puts twist into the line. There are things you can do to avoid line twist:

- *When putting line on a reel always use a pen or screwdriver to hold the spool and let line flow off the spool in a straight line. Don't wind the line off the side with the spool laying flat on the ground.*
- *Always have the drag correctly set. Every time you hear the drag click over while you are turning the handle of the reel you are putting twist into the line.*
- *The same applies when you are fighting a fish, don't just wind the reel against drag. Lift the rod and wind as you lower it. (See Fighting and Landing a Fish Chapter xx). If the drag is squawking you should not be winding.*
- *Watch if your bait spins a lot when you wind it in. Try to minimise this twisting, by keeping the bait straight.*
- *Where possible, use very small swivels to help reduce line twist.*

To remove twist from a line, the easiest way is to cut the rig off and pay out the twisted portion of the line behind a boat moving at 6 to 10 knots. All the twist will be removed from the line in a few minutes.

Land-based anglers can tie on a small ball sinker and trim the knot. Cast this out into deep water but keep the sinker off the bottom. The line twist will quickly spin out of the line.

fishing rigs: The swivel acts as the connector between main line and leader, or as the stopper for the sinker in many rigs.

Lure fishermen use a swivel with a snap attached to enable them to change lures quickly but very securely. However, snap swivels should not be used for bait fishing as they tend to tangle easily in these rigs.

Swivels also come in a range of designs, with the brass barrel type being the most common and popular type. Ball-bearing swivels are used in blue-water fishing to handle the extra weight of big fish. When using swivels always choose the smallest sizes that will still get the job done because this keeps your rigs streamlined.

Various snap styles

Crosslock snap

Hawaiian snap   Coastlock snap

Interlock snap

Speed clip

Snap system snap

Hook snap

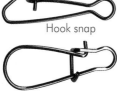

Doulock snap

ANADROMOUS FISH

Most saltwater fish can't survive in fresh water, nor can most freshwater fish live in the ocean. Certain species, however, spend time in each environment and are described as "anadromous."

Fish such as American shad, striped bass and salmon begin life as eggs that hatch in freshwater rivers. Some species spend just a few months in fresh water while others live in rivers for a year or more. As the young fish grow, they follow the river downstream and eventually swim out to the ocean. They spend several years in the sea, where they continue to grow and mature.

When it is time to spawn (lay eggs), anadromous fish swim upriver to reproduce and complete their life cycle. Shad and striped bass can spawn repeatedly throughout their lifespan but salmon spawn only once. Both males and females die after fulfilling the mating ritual. Driven by instinct and guided by a highly developed sense of smell, salmon travel hundreds of miles through the ocean to locate the river in which they were hatched years before. They return to swim upstream, lay eggs and die in the same river where they were born.

Biologists discovered that the decaying flesh from dead, spawned-out salmon stimulates the growth of microorganisms in the rivers and contributes to the survival of the next generation of salmon. Upon hatching in the spring, salmon fry feed on these microorganisms. In nature, nothing goes to waste!

Salmon swimming upstream to spawn.

Wherever possible keep your tackle in boxes by fishing type or for specific fish and keep the tckle separated so that all of one size and type is by itself.

LEADERS

A leader is the piece of line or wire between the hook and the main line. The leader is usually a piece of monofilament stronger than the main line that helps stop abrasion and break-offs from the fish's teeth, gill covers or body. Leaders are also used when fishing in areas where there may be oyster-covered rocks or submerged timber. A wire leader prevents sharp-toothed fish such as northern pike and bluefish from cutting the line.

Sometimes the leader is made of lighter line to help with presentation to very shy fish. It is very difficult for fish to see a leader lighter than the main line, so you have a better chance of getting a bite. This particularly applies to fish like trout. Just remember to set the drag and fight the fish according to the lighter leader strength.

In other fishing situations, the leader consists of the same material as the main line. For example, when fishing for bass, carp or small catfish, a special leader is not required. Just use your main line to make the rig. This is common practice.

Always remember that leaders are extremely important because they are the link between you and the hooked fish. Pay attention to tying the knots

HINT BOX

Storing terminal tackle

Terminal tackle is the term given to the equipment that you tie on to the end of your line—hooks, sinkers, swivels etc. Good quality terminal tackle is by no means cheap and, due to its size, is one of the easiest items of tackle to misplace. The best approach for storing small tackle items is to set aside a separate tackle box that fits inside your creel, basket or main tackle box.

A variety of boxes with individual compartments are available on the market. These allow for each item of terminal tackle to be stored in its own individual area.

FISH FACT

PHOTO: ROBERT FULTON JNR

NESTING SUNFISH

In the springtime look carefully in the shallows of a lake and you may see fish suspended over small, bowl-shaped depressions. These are nesting sunfish. Male sunfish (including bass, bluegill, pumpkinseed and crappie) build nests in which the females lay eggs. The males then guard the nest, chasing away fish and salamanders that try to steal the eggs or eat the newly hatched fry.

HINT BOX

Wire leaders for bluefish

Bluefish can sever monofilament line with their sharp teeth, yet surprisingly few bite-offs occur when fishing with lures. This is largely because the fish's tail-biting attack generally results in a lip or mouth hook-up that leaves it chewing on hook shanks or the lure's body.

However large bluefish can easily engulf a lure or bait, and if you expect to encounter fish over 4 pounds, use a short length of light wire for good insurance. Wire may also be needed when using live baits or fish strips on single hooks.

RINGS

Two types of rings are used in fishing, split rings and solid brass rings.

Split rings are used on lures to enable the fitting and changing of hooks. They are made of either stainless steel or nickel-plated steel.

Solid brass rings are just a little circle of solid brass. These rings are used in rigs as a strong connector, particularly in big-game fishing or when using heavy lines.

Rings make great connectors. Line to line or hook to lure.

correctly and make sure this vital part of the rig is right. The best and most appropriate knots to tie for each part of the leader are shown in chapter 3 of this book, along with detailed tying diagrams and instructions.

did you know ...

TEETH OF A SHARK

Different kinds of sharks have different shaped teeth and this is one of the characteristics that scientist use to distinguish among various species.

Tiger sharks have triangular shaped teeth. This allows them to feed on a broad range of prey.

The great white shark also has triangular shaped teeth that are much bigger than those of the other sharks. When the jaw closes the upper and lower teeth act like serrated scissors.

The mako shark has slender teeth that help it grasp its prey, allowing the shark to swallow its meal whole.

There are many other species of sharks in Australia and all have specific shaped teeth to help them with their particular feeding method

LINES

Fishing lines have all sorts of characteristics that affect their performance: breaking strength, stretch, color, softness, diameter and so on. Of these, breaking strength and diameter rank as most important.

Breaking strength and diameter

It is not valid to talk about breaking strength without looking at the

diameter of the line as well. Different brands have different diameter lines for the same breaking strain and each has its uses. It is necessary to choose what will best suit the type of fishing you do.

The line size must also suit the reel. Putting 40-pound line on a small spinning reel will just about stop you from casting any distance because it's just too heavy. The line must also sit well on the reel and cope with wear and tear and the line strength must comfortably handle the average fish being sought.

You will generally catch more fish by using lighter lines but it must be kept in perspective; don't go too light or you might get broken off easily. For most freshwater fishing, 6 to 8 pound breaking strength is ideal. Surfcasters normally use 12 to 20 pound line while offshore anglers use 30 to 50 pound line.

Thin lines cast better than thick lines and allow you to cast light lures and baits with greater ease.

So when you compare fishing lines, look at both the breaking strength and the diameter. The

HINT BOX

Matching line and casting weight

It is important that the line's breaking strength matches the weight of the lure or sinker and bait you're using. The rule says, light sinker or lure, light line. Use the following table as a guide.

Breaking strength	Optimum casting weight
2 pound-test	$1/10$ to $1/3$ ounce
4 pound-test	$1/3$ to $1/2$ ounce
6 pound-test	$1/2$ to $2/3$ ounce
8 pound-test	$2/3$- to 1 ounce
10 pound-test	1 to $1 1/4$ ounce
12 pound-test	1 to $1 2/3$ ounce
14 pound-test	1 to $1 2/3$ ounce
16 pound-test	1 to 2 ounce
20 pound-test	$1 1/2$ to 3 ounce
30 pound-test	2 to $4 1/4$ ounce
50 pound-test	3 to 7 ounce

diameter will be shown in inches or millimeters. The average 6-pound line has a .009-inch diameter (0.25 mm) while a thin line of the same strength measures .008 inches (0.20 mm) or even ,007 inches (0.18 mm). The only drawback here is that ultra thin lines tend to cost a lot of money. It is often better to stay with a good quality, medium thickness line than to pay huge amounts for very thin lines.

The softness of the line lets it sit snugly on the reel while the stretch adds a type of shock-absorber effect when fighting a fish. All monofilament fishing lines stretch when under load.

Memory in fishing lines refers to the coils it can form from being wound onto a spool under tension. Some lines retain these coils, which can be very annoying to anglers.

Fishing lines can be colored for various reasons. Deep-sea anglers often use bright yellow lines so the skipper can see them easily against a blue sea while fighting a fish. Anglers chasing shy fish like trout and tuna prefer more natural colors like green, brown or blue so the line fades into the background. For most fishing, choose lines with a natural or neutral color as these usually produce the best results.

Braided lines

Braided fishing lines are very popular in many forms of fishing. These lines have a very low diameter for a given strength, often measuring only half or one third as thick as monofilament line of the same strength. They also have little or no stretch and so transmit the sensation of every bite or strike very directly to the angler.

Braided lines are used extensively by anglers fishing deep water. This thin line generates less resistance through the water and is less affected by current. Bite sensitivity is also increased as is the ability to firmly set the hook.

Anglers who cast and troll lures also use braid because of its sensitivity and instant hook-up capacity. The fine diameter of the line allows the easy casting of small lures and soft-plastic jigs.

The only down side to braided lines is the cost. They are very expensive when compared to monofilament.

Fact Box

LATERAL LINE

The lateral line, which runs along the side of a fish, is actually a collection of sensitive receptors that can pick up minute vibrations. It allows fish to hear and feel things moving in the water.

The lateral line assists fish in keeping together in schools without touching when they cannot see each other at night. During the day, vision may play a large part in this, but at night, each fish responds to the water pressure caused by another fish moving toward or beside it so that all the fish in a school move in unison.

BOBBERS

Bobbers, sometimes called floats, serve several roles for the angler. A bobber floats on the surface and suspends bait at a desired depth where the angler believes fish will be feeding. This depth can be easily adjusted with most bobbers. The bobber is also a bite indicator because its movement tells the angler when a fish takes the bait.

Bobbers come in a very wide variety of shapes and sizes to suit all sorts of fish and fishing situations. Most floats are made from buoyant material including foam, plastic, cork, wood and even porcupine quills. They also come in a range of colors to help the angler see them when fishing. Light colors are used for still, dark waters and red, orange or yellow for choppy or turbulent conditions.

Types of bobbers

Round Plastic Bobber: Available in a wide range of sizes, these popular, easy-to-use bobbers attach to the line via spring-loaded clips. They can be locked in place or rigged as slip bobbers.

Pencil Bobber: Favored by panfishermen, pencil bobbers are extremely sensitive and reveal the lightest bites.

Casting Bubble: These round or football-shaped floats are often chosen by trout anglers or panfishermen who want to use very light artificials, such as flies, on spinning tackle. Plugs or holes allow the float to be partially filled with water, which serves as the casting weight.

Sliding or Slip Bobber: Designed to run freely up and down the line and stop at a particular depth, sliding bobbers prove especially useful in deeper water. They give greater distance and accuracy in casting than most other designs.

Chum Bobber: These bobbers or bobber attachments are filled with chum, which then slowly enters the water around the baited hook (See Chapter 4 page 37). Chum bobbers are very useful for carp fishing.

Popping Cork: Most often used in saltwater for redfish and seatrout, these floats have a concave face that makes a loud "pop" when the angler pulls the line sharply. The noise attracts fish, which then take the bait.

Rigging a bobber

Most bobbers are designed to ride upright in the water. If after casting you find that the bobber lays on its side, it either needs more lead or the lead is set too deeply and is resting on the bottom. It may also be tangled.

No matter what type of bobber you use, it should be balanced to sit the way you want it. This balance is provided by using split shot or small sinkers to achieve the desired result. As a rule, fish should be able to pull the bobber under the water with very little resistance, so the bobber should be weighted to sit mostly below the surface.

The point at which the bobber is suspended is set by using a stopper, which is usually small and soft enough to pass easily through the rod guides. Most tackle shops sell bobber stops which are designed to slide onto your line and they make the job of fitting a stopper as simple as possible. The stopper needs to be large enough to stop the float moving past the desired depth, but small enough to pass through the rod guides.

When to strike

Part of the fun of using a bobber comes from seeing what is happening with your bait. Watching the bobber carefully tells you exactly what's going on beneath the surface. All you need to do is set the hook at the right time to catch the fish.

When the float bobs up and down it means something is attacking the bait. If it goes under or moves steadily in one direction it usually means the fish has shown a definite interest and has taken the bait.

Different types of fish will take the bait in different ways. Sunfish and bass usually feed aggressively. When fishing for these with small, soft baits and little hooks a quick strike is usually needed. Carp and trout are often far more cautious about the bait and need a little time to take it properly.

Pike and large bass taking a live minnow fished under a bobber will usually consume the bait whole and will be hooked as soon as you raise the rod to set the hook.

TACKLE BOX

Everyone needs a tackle box of some kind to store the gear they take fishing. For some anglers it is just a plastic container with some hooks, sinkers and swivels. For others, it's a multi-shelf, flip-top, high-tech mobile tackle shop. Most anglers just need something that keeps their essential gear neatly ordered, protects it from the elements and is easy to carry around.

The contents of your tackle box will depend on the type of fishing you prefer, but most anglers need the following standard equipment.

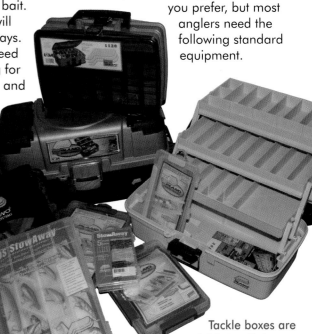

Tackle boxes are available in all shapes, sizes and materials. Select one that holds all of your tackle for a specific fish species or method of fishing.

Hooks

Hooks are best stored in a small, plastic containers within the tackle box. Little plastic boxes with clear lids are ideal for keeping hooks organized and preventing them from scattering if the tackle box falls over. Storing them in a small box also helps keep them dry, which prevents rusting.

Carry only enough hooks for a couple of trips. If you carry lots of hooks around they'll mostly end up rusty.

Sinkers

Sinkers are heavy! Packing too many of them will make your tackle box uncomfortable to carry. So, just as with hooks, carry only what you will need for a couple of trips. Keep the sinkers in the bottom of the tackle box. If you put them in the shelves they tend to unbalance the box when you open it. The smaller sinkers can be placed in the tackle compartment box with your hooks.

Swivels

Keep these small items in compartments with lids to prevent scattering. Twenty or so should be plenty.

Knife

Choose a knife that has a scaler on the back, It will make cleaning fish easier and saves carrying a separate scaler. A knife is an essential fishing tool used for cutting bait, trimming knots, cleaning fish and other odd jobs. Keep your knife clean and sharp but always take care when using it.

Sharpening stone

A small, fine grained carborundum stone is necessary to keep both your knife and hooks sharp.

Pliers

A pair of long-nosed pliers is needed for crimping sinkers onto the line, trimming knots, cutting wire, tuning lures and removing hooks from fish with teeth. Store pliers in the bottom of the tackle box.

Cutters

A pair of sharp cutters are a great working tool when making rigs and trimming line. They are a neat, cheap and safe way to work with line.

Lures

Lures are like hooks: Carry only what you need and what works where you are going to fish. It is pointless carry around large bass plugs if you are

fishing a small stream for trout. In this case you would just need a few spinners and small spoons.

Ruler or measure

Always carry something to measure your fish. It is important that you do not keep undersized fish, so a ruler can be a handy guide. Some tackle stores have stick-on labels in the form of a ruler that can be applied to the outside of your tackle box to save space.

Spare line

A spool of spare line is always handy. Anglers can often lose a bit of line to snags, tangles or even a big fish. Having a spare spool of line means you can just splice the lines, top off your reel and keep fishing. The spare spool can also be used as a handline if you need it.

did you know ...

AIR BLADDER

A fish's air bladder (also called gas bladder or swim bladder) is a gas-filled sac located in the middle-dorsal section of its body. The air bladder provides an internal float to keep the fish at a constant depth in the water without the necessity for the fish to be constantly swimming.

A fish regulates the amount of air in the bladder when it wants to rise or descend in the water. The gas is usually a mixture of oxygen and nitrogen. Sudden changes of depth can cause the bladder to expand quickly and the stomach or bladder may be pushed out of the fish's mouth by the pressure. This can be seen when deep-water fish are hauled to the surface.

Some fish lack swim bladders. Saltwater bottom-dwelling species like flounder have no need of one. However, surface and midwater species without air bladders, including tuna, swordfish, marlin and sharks must remain constantly in motion to avoid sinking.

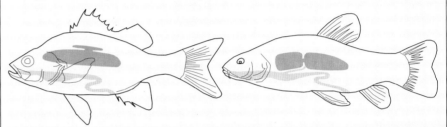

The air bladders of the tench (right) and perch (left). In species such as tench, carp, trout and freshwater salmon, there is a duct that links the air bladder to the intestinal tract, enabling the fish to absorb and release air directly through the mouth. In perch-like fish, this duct is absent and the fish relies on glands to absorb and secrete gas.

Fact Box

Pocket Guides

Many anglers carry a pocket guide or fisheries booklet with them to help identify fish they've caught or refer to regulations. A small tide table is also very useful and these are normally available free from most good tackle shops.

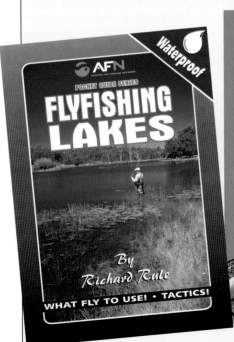

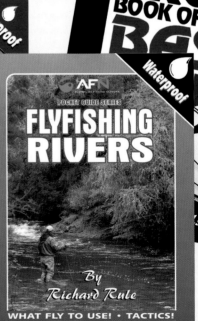

CHAPTER 2

CASTING

Two things are important when casting: distance and accuracy. In most situations, accuracy is the more important of the two.
To achieve both distance and accuracy, the tackle must be properly balanced and maintained. The reel should be correctly filled with line and the rod must be appropriate for the style of fishing you'll do. Get the tackle right, and the rest is up to you.

Casting accuracy is essential to success. Using artificials for trout, bass, bluefish and even tuna demands precise lure presentation. Anglers fishing with bait also need to be very particular about where and how they cast. In all situations, even surfcasting and pier fishing, anglers should cast to specific targets rather than just lobbing out baits anywhere.

Good casting develops with practice; books like this and others only give the theory and some guidelines. When casting, always concentrate on what you are doing and try to get it right. If the cast goes too high, it's because you released the line too early. If the bait or lure slams into the water close by, the release was too late.

fact Box

KEEP IT TOPPED UP

The quantity of line on the reel spool directly affects both casting distance and retrieve speed. Think of it this way: Low amounts of line equal low performance.

Any reel that is low on line will not cast well, especially spinning reels. Casting with a small amount of line on the reel causes the line to hit the lip of the spool as it goes out. This creates excessive friction, slows down the line and results in drastically reduced casting distance.

Baitcasting reels lose casting distance when they get low on line because the spool has to spin much faster and line doesn't flow off the reel as smoothly.

The amount of line on the spool also influences how quickly you recover line with each turn of the handle. The more line on a reel, the greater the spool size and the faster the retrieve. If the spool is only 75-percent filled, you will lose 25 percent of the retrieve speed.

All anglers should keep their reels full of line to ensure maximum performance from their tackle.

Work on getting a smooth flow of energy through the rod and into the cast. Don't force it, though. Trying too hard only causes more problems. Start with short casts and work up from there.

Once you achieve a comfortable casting style, both distance and accuracy will improve as long as you keep practicing and working at it.

Remember, all tackle has its limits and you can only achieve results within the capacity of the gear. Also, peak accuracy occurs at about 80 percent of maximum casting distance (it's harder to hit targets that are very close or very far away). Keep this in mind when casting to spots at different distances.

Learn to use a variety of casting styles. You should be able to cast from both the right- and left-hand sides and from directly overhead. This is particularly important when working in crowds, from a small boat or on a tree-lined shore.

In the end, good casting should become a reflex action with the bait or lure going exactly where you want it to. Don't be afraid to make mistakes, it all takes time and practice.

Matching the casting weight to the tackle is also very important. For example, it is impossible to cast a small, light spinner on a heavy-action baitcasting outfit loaded with 30-pound line. Casting tiny lures calls for 4- or 6-pound line, a light-action rod and matching spinning reel.

You'll find that balanced tackle makes fishing much easier and enjoyable. Choose a rod, reel, line and lures or bait that work together smoothly.

HINT BOX

Iron out casting problems

When your reel is full of line and the rod, reel and casting weight are properly matched, the rest is up to the angler.

While most people learn to cast as part of a day's fishing, casting can be improved with a little specific practice.

Find an open area with no trees overhead and no snags in the water, and try a little casting practice. Pay attention to how the cast is affected when you change things like the amount of power you apply, sinker sizes, the way you release the line and when you release it.

Just take the time to get it right. Like any other sport, the more casting you do the easier and more natural it gets.

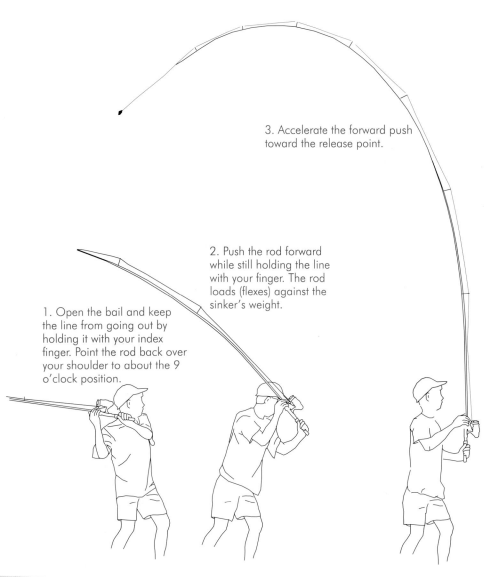

3. Accelerate the forward push toward the release point.

2. Push the rod forward while still holding the line with your finger. The rod loads (flexes) against the sinker's weight.

1. Open the bail and keep the line from going out by holding it with your index finger. Point the rod back over your shoulder to about the 9 o'clock position.

Casting a two-handed surf outfit.
Apply power by pushing forward with the top hand (the right hand in the case of right-handed anglers) and pulling back toward the body with the left hand, held low on the rod butt.

4. As the rod approaches vertical, straighten your finger to release the line. Follow through with the cast, lowering the rod tip and pointing it toward the target as line flows off the reel.

CHAPTER 3

KNOTS & RIGS

Knowing how to choose and tie reliable knots is an essential part of fishing that can confuse those who are just getting started. Fortunately, a number of knots are quite easy to tie and they work very well in a wide variety of situations. In this chapter we teach you how to tie essential knots and show how and where to use them when rigging terminal tackle.

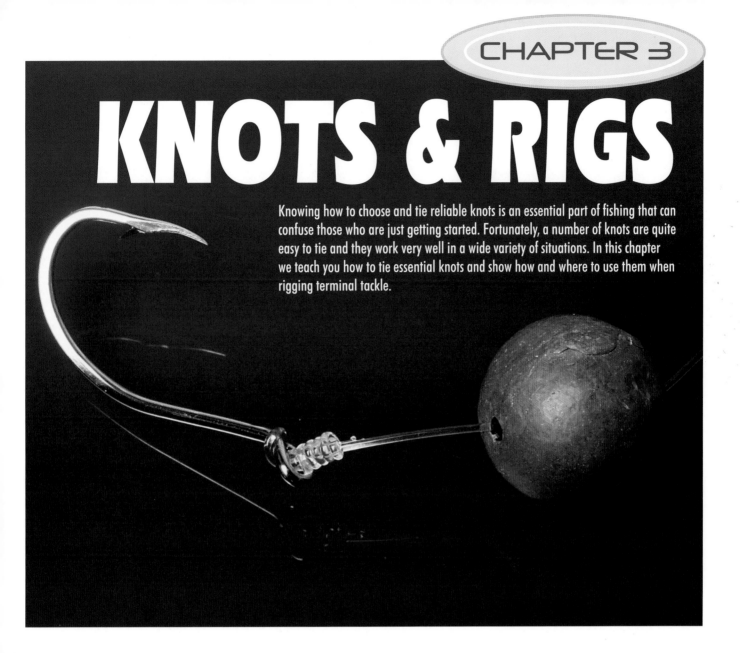

KNOTS

Whether you fish in fresh water or salt water, there are only a few basic knots you really need to master.

For tying hooks, swivels and rings to monofilament, two simple and effective knots will serve you well: the improved clinch knot and the uni-knot. Practice tying both, then decide which one you feel most comfortable using. Surfcasters, pier fishermen and freshwater bottomfishermen rely on the blood bight dropper knot to create a loop for attaching sinkers and hooks to a rig.

When you're ready to tie on a plug and give lure fishing a whirl, study the Lefty's loop. It's essential to use a loop knot when attaching

lures because plugs, crankbaits and jigs deliver much better fish-catching action with the freedom of movement the loop provides. Sometimes you need to attach a leader to your main line, especially when targeting large fish, trolling or surfcasting. The Albright knot provides the easiest, most secure way to connect two lines of different breaking strengths.

A couple other knots come in handy for special situations. The arbor knot rates as a simple and reliable way to anchor line on a reel prior to spooling up. Braided "superlines" seem to become more popular every day. They work best in conjunction with monofilament leaders, which make it easier to change lures or rigs.

Braided line's very thin diameter and smooth surface often cause knots to slip and come undone, but a carefully tied double uni-knot firmly joins line and leader in this case.

When tying knots, always lubricate them with a small amount of saliva before pulling them tight. Cinching down on dry fishing line creates friction that can scorch the line and weaken the knot.

Learning to tie these knots properly takes some time. Start practicing now so you can use them to build the rigs described in this book. In knot-tying terms, "standing line" refers to the main line going back to the reel, and "tag end" refers to the line's free end.

Improved Clinch Knot

This simple yet strong knot is very good for attaching hooks and snap swivels to your line.

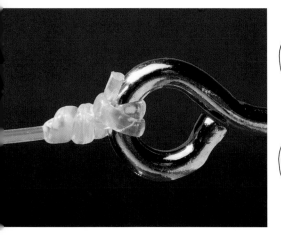

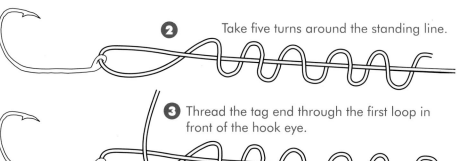

1 Thread the line in the hook eye and pull to get a few inches of tag end.

2 Take five turns around the standing line.

3 Thread the tag end through the first loop in front of the hook eye.

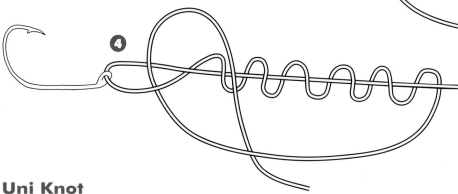

4 Thread the tag end through the large loop just formed. Wet the knot and pull steadily on the standing line to cinch the knot against the hook. Trim the tag and you're done.

Uni Knot

Another simple, strong knot for attaching terminal tackle.

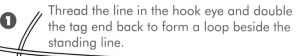

1 Thread the line in the hook eye and double the tag end back to form a loop beside the standing line.

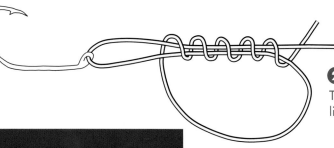

2 Take four turns around both strands of line inside the loop.

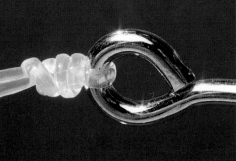

3 Wet the line and close the knot but don't cinch it down completely.

4 Slide the knot against the hook eye, pull it tight and trim the tag.

Fact Box

ENEMIES OF NYLON LINE

Nylon fishing line has a number of enemies, the worst being abrasion, poorly-tied knots and sunlight.

Abrasion

Sand, rocks, barnacles, faulty rod guides and other obstacles can give lines a tough time. Take care to avoid dragging your line over rough surfaces. You should also check that the reel's bail arm roller or levelwind carrier is smooth and in good condition to minimize abrasion. Abrasion weakens line and can cause it to break suddenly.

Bad knots

Lines have good strength provided the knots you tie carefully and correctly. Always take care to tie good knots and lubricate them with saliva as they are tightened.

Sunlight

Although it happens very slowly, the ultraviolet rays in sunlight weaken fishing line. The effect of the sun from a day's fishing is small and unavoidable, but don't store reels at home where they will be in direct sunlight for an extended time. Keeping your reels and extra spools of line in a dark place, such as in the basement, helps them stay strong and last longer.

Blood Bight Dropper Knot

This knot is used to make loops that stand off the main line, to which you can attach your hooks. Additionally you can tie a Blood Bight at the end of the rig and use it to attach your sinkers. This is a very important knot when making rigs to fish off piers, rocks, surf and jetties. It is also used when bottom fishing offshore and in bays.

Double the line back to make a loop of the size desired.

Bring the end of the loop twice over the doubled part.

Now pass the end of the loop through the first loop formed in the doubled part.

Draw the knot up into shape, keeping the pressure on both lines.

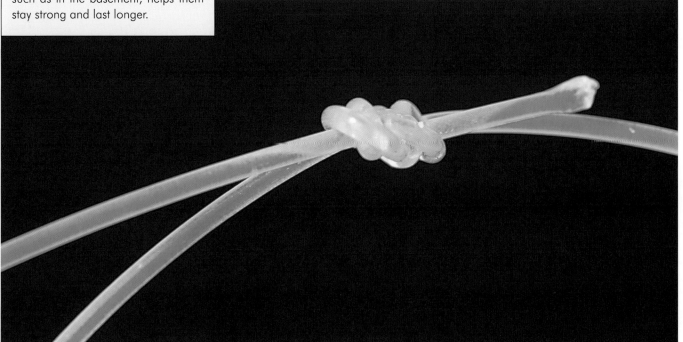

Leftys Loop

This knot is about the easiest of the
lure loop knots to master and is
equally effective on light or heavy
lines. When locked it doesn't slip and
it has a very high knot strength, well
over 90 percent, so it can be used
with leaders or just straight onto the
main line.

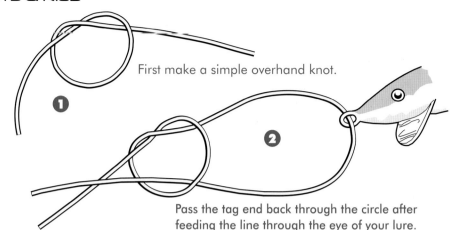

❶ First make a simple overhand knot.

❷ Pass the tag end back through the circle after
feeding the line through the eye of your lure.

Wrap the main line with the tag
about 3–5 times

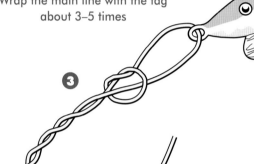

❸

Feed the tag through
the first wrap of your
original overhand
knot.

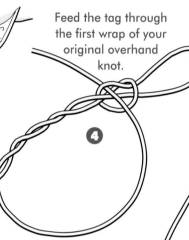

❹

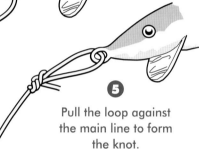

❺

Pull the loop against
the main line to form
the knot.

Albright Knot

The Albright knot serves to join
two monofilament lines of different
diameters, such as when attaching a
heavier leader to your main line. DO
NOT use the Albight to tie a mono
leader to superbraid line because the
knot may slip!

❶

Form a loop in the end of the heavier line
by bending back about 5 inches of line. Pass
the tag end of the lighter line through this
loop.

Pinch the lines about 3 inches from the
end of the loop, leaving about 3 inches
of tag beyond this point to tie the knot.

❷

❸

Working down toward the loop,
take 10 wraps around all three
strands of line. Pass the tag end
through the end loop on the same
side it originally entered.

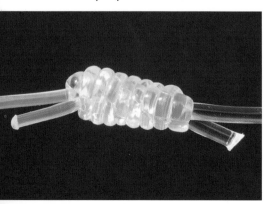

Slowly pull both strands of lighter line while
grasping the heavier line and working the knot's
coils toward the loop end. Do not let the coils slip
off the loop. Tighten, then trim the tag ends.

❹

Thumb Knot

This is the knot to use with 60- to 200-pound-test monofilament. It may be that you are live baiting for tuna or grouper or trolling offshore with big lures. With really heavy monofilament you need a knot that allows you to tighten and lock it. The locked half blood and uni knots are not suitable here.

This is an optional knot to learn and only needed if you require a rig in the following section that specifies this knot.

1 Thread your hook with the line and make a loop so that the hook is suspended from the loop. Pinch the crossover between the thumb and finger of your left hand. Start wrapping your left thumb and loop with the tag. Make three wraps in all, working from the base of your thumb toward the thumbnail.

2 Push the tag back under those three wraps alongside your thumb. Push it all the way back toward the base of your thumb. Secure the tag against your left thumb with your middle finger.

3 Then take the hook loop in your right hand and ease the wraps off your thumb, one at a time in sequence.

4 Close the knot by exerting pressure on the loop against the tag.

Double Uni Knot

The double uni quickly and effectively joins two lines. It's ideal for attaching a monofilament leader to superbraid line because it won't slip when tied correctly.

1 Run the lines to be joined parallel and then take one tag end and form a loop over the other line.

2 Wrap the tag through the loop and around the lines four or five times.

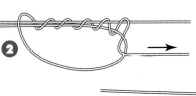

3 Draw the knot together.

4 Repeat the process with the other tag end.

5 Lubricate both knots and then pull them together.

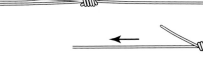

6 Then take the tag ends to clinch the knots tight. Pull on the lines again to ensure that the knots are snug. Trim off the tags.

Arbor Knot

This is a very fast and secure knot for attaching line to the reel.

Pass the tag end of the line around the spool and form an overhand knot with the tag end around the main line. Then tie another overhand knot on the tag end of the line.

Lubricate the knots, tighten down by pulling the main line and trim the tag.

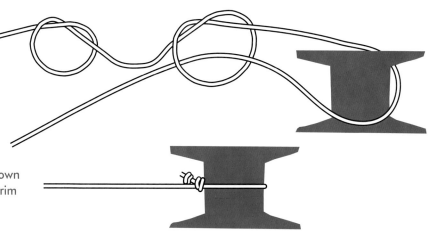

RIGS

Rigs are the business end of fishing tackle. A good rig presents bait naturally, in a way fish find attractive.

The rigs shown here work well and are proven fish catchers, and are a good starting point for those new to fishing. When constructing these rigs, keep in mind two important points: tie good knots and use sharp hooks.

Use the appropriate knots for each rig and tie them well. Poorly tied knots may slip out or weaken the line, resulting in lost fish.

The final part of the rig is the hook. Select hooks of the right size for the fish you are chasing and make sure they are sharp. Needle-sharp hooks penetrate and hold fish better than dull ones.

FRESHWATER RIGS

In many cases, rigging for freshwater fishing means tying on a hook and perhaps pinching a split shot or two on the line for casting weight. This no-nonsense setup works perfectly when drifting bait for trout in streams or dunking worms for bluegill in a lake.

You're better off keeping things as simple as possible, but sometimes you need to fine-tune rigs for certain situations.

Dropper Rig

This basic bottomfishing rig works in rivers as well as lakes. Use it with all kinds of baits (live minnows, worms, doughballs, corn) for trout, bass, catfish and other fish. Choose a

sinker that's just big enough to hold bottom and a hook that matches your target species.

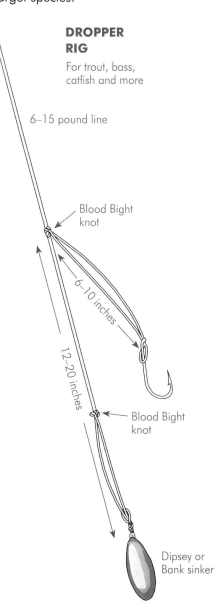

DROPPER RIG

For trout, bass, catfish and more

6–15 pound line

Blood Bight knot

6–10 inches

12–20 inches

Blood Bight knot

Dipsey or Bank sinker

Light Slip-Sinker Rig

Another easy-to-make bottomfishing rig, this one proves especially effective on sensitive feeders like carp. They can mouth the bait without feeling the sinker's weight. The slip-sinker rig also works well when drifting live minnows and worms for walleye and bass. Use a sinker just heavy enough to maintain contact with the bottom without hanging up.

Heavy Slip-Sinker Rig

Use this rig when presenting bulky baits, such as chunks of shad or whole sunfish, to large customers like blue and flathead catfish. Use a sinker just heavy enough to maintain contact with the bottom without hanging up.

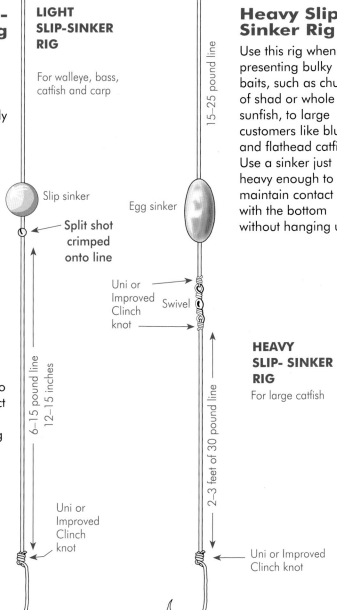

LIGHT SLIP-SINKER RIG

For walleye, bass, catfish and carp

Slip sinker

Split shot crimped onto line

6–15 pound line

12–15 inches

Uni or Improved Clinch knot

15–25 pound line

Egg sinker

Uni or Improved Clinch knot

Swivel

HEAVY SLIP-SINKER RIG

For large catfish

2–3 feet of 30 pound line

Uni or Improved Clinch knot

HINT BOX

Stalking the fish

Many fish feed and are caught in shallow, often clear water. Approaching these fish and presenting a bait or lure to them demands a level of hunting skill called "stalking." Experienced anglers try to sneak up on the fish. They move slowly and deliberately, using polarized sunglasses to cut the water's glare and see where fish are holding.

When stream fishing, always keep well back from the water to avoid spooking wary fish. Stay low and look for rocks and bushes that can give you cover. Work the fishiest areas with as little disturbance as possible before moving up to the water's edge.

When wading, walk slowly and make sure your foothold is good.

In a boat, always slow down before reaching the fishing area and idle in or use an electric motor or oars for a really quiet approach.

Fixed-Bobber Rig

Baits suspended at mid depths attract trout, bass and sunfish. Crappie fishermen often use bobbers to present small jigs at precise depths. A plastic clip-on bobber is perfect for a fixed-bobber rig that hold baits within 1 to 3 feet of the surface.

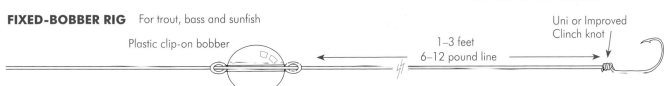

FIXED-BOBBER RIG   For trout, bass and sunfish

Plastic clip-on bobber

Uni or Improved Clinch knot

1–3 feet
6–12 pound line

Slip-Bobber Rig

Use a slip-bobber setup when you want to suspend baits farther below the surface. The bobber slides to the end of the line for easy casting, then the stop controls how deep the bait goes.

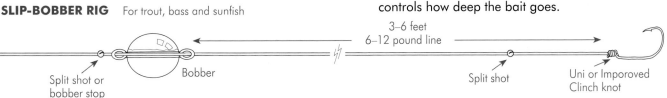

SLIP-BOBBER RIG   For trout, bass and sunfish

Split shot or bobber stop

Bobber

3–6 feet
6–12 pound line

Split shot

Uni or Imporoved Clinch knot

SALTWATER RIGS

SURFCASTING RIGS
Surfcasting Dropper Rig
Make this rig with one, two or three droppers and bait the hooks with bloodworms, clams or shrimp to catch fish along the beach. The pyramid sinker facilitates long casts and holds in sandy bottom so wave action doesn't carry the line to shore.

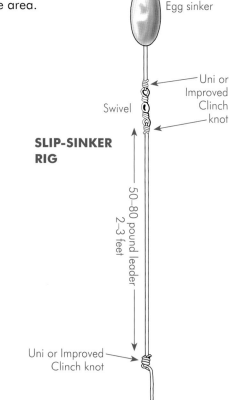

10–20 pound line
Blood Bight knot
12 inches
8 inches
Blood Bight knot
8 inches
12 inches
Blood Bight knot
12 inches
8 inches
Blood Bight knot
Pyramid sinker

SURFCASTING DROPPER RIG

CLOSE SURFCASTING RIG

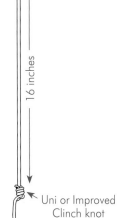

Blood Bight knot
8 inches
12–20 pound line
12 inches
slip sinker
Uni or Improved Clinch knot
Swivel
16 inches
Uni or Improved Clinch knot

Close Surfcasting Rig
When fish move in to feed right in the surf zone, use this rig to let baits roll in the waves for a natural presentation. Use just enough weight to hold bottom, and make sure the hook sizes match the fish in the area.

RIGS FOR BAYS AND SHALLOW WATER
Slip-Sinker Rig
You can use this rig for working from mid depths all the way down to the bottom. Since it allows more freedom of movement than the dropper rig, the slip-sinker rig is the way to go when fishing with live bait. Sinker size determines how fast your bait sinks and how deep it goes. You'll need a wire leader if bluefish or mackerel are in the area.

HINT BOX
Make every rig count
Tie every rig you make—no matter what its intended use—as if the fish of a lifetime will be hooked on it. All too often a large fish grabs a bait intended for smaller quarry. If you have been haphazard in tying your knots, chances are you and that trophy fish will quickly part company. On the other hand, if each knot is carefully tied and the line checked for damage, you have the best chance of success.

Some incredibly big fish have been landed on very light line and tiny hooks by anglers with the right combination of cool-headedness, patience, skill, luck and attention to detail in their rigging.

15–30 pound line
Egg sinker
Uni or Improved Clinch knot
Swivel

SLIP-SINKER RIG

50–80 pound leader 2–3 feet
Uni or Improved Clinch knot

Popping-Cork Rig

A favorite among shallow-water anglers, this rig is deadly on speckled trout and redfish. The noisy cork calls them in, then the fish take the shrimp or jig they see dangling before their nose.

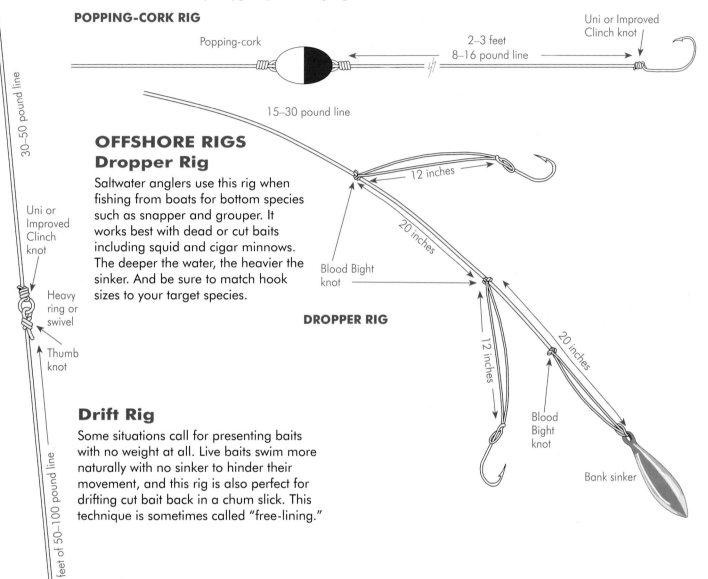

POPPING-CORK RIG

Popping-cork

2–3 feet
8–16 pound line

Uni or Improved
Clinch knot

15–30 pound line

30–50 pound line

Uni or
Improved
Clinch
knot

Heavy
ring or
swivel

Thumb
knot

OFFSHORE RIGS
Dropper Rig

Saltwater anglers use this rig when fishing from boats for bottom species such as snapper and grouper. It works best with dead or cut baits including squid and cigar minnows. The deeper the water, the heavier the sinker. And be sure to match hook sizes to your target species.

DROPPER RIG

12 inches

20 inches

Blood Bight
knot

12 inches

20 inches

Blood
Bight
knot

Bank sinker

Drift Rig

Some situations call for presenting baits with no weight at all. Live baits swim more naturally with no sinker to hinder their movement, and this rig is also perfect for drifting cut bait back in a chum slick. This technique is sometimes called "free-lining."

60 feet of 50–100 pound line

**DRIFT
RIG**

Thumb
knot

6/0–8/0
Game
hook

Fact Box

HOOKS MADE OF WIRE

Most fish hooks are made of wire that has been cut to size then shaped by special machines. Modern technology produces perfectly shaped and very sharp hooks at high speeds. Only forged big-game hooks are made differently. The specific type of wire used gives each hook many of its individual characteristics. Different mixtures of metal in the wire make hooks either soft or hard (this is known as the temper of the metal).

The wire is also coated with various substances to give hooks a colored finish and a degree of rust resistance. The hook coating is usually indicated on the box they come in. Read the label and you will see names like bronzed, nickel coated, cadmium, tinned and so on to indicate the coating.

PIER AND JETTY RIGS
Pier Dropper Rig

This simple but effective rig is easy to prepare and gets results. Use dead baits such as fish chunks or shrimp and heave it out there!

General Rig

This all-around rig works with live or dead bait, and the long leader allows baits more movement than a dropper rig.

PIER DROPPER RIG

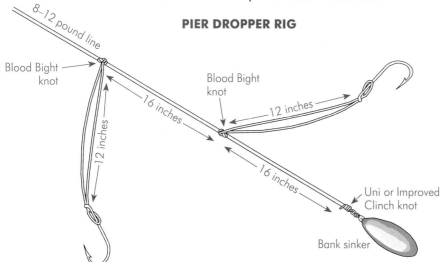

8–12 pound line

Blood Bight knot

Blood Bight knot

16 inches

12 inches

12 inches

16 inches

12 inches

Uni or Improved Clinch knot

Bank sinker

12–20 pound line

Egg sinker

Uni or Improved Clinch knot

Swivel

16–20 inches of 16–30 pound line

GENERAL RIG

Uni or Improved Clinch knot

Anglers try their luck on a pier.

HOOK GUIDE

You can use just about any type of hook when making rigs as long as the size matches your target species. Keep in mind, however, that certain hook styles and shapes perform better with different kinds of bait. For example, the tiny barbs on a baitholder's shank keep worms from slipping off the hook, while a fine-wire Aberdeen hook is perfect for delicate baits like crickets.

One style may go by several different names, depending on the manufacturer. You may see kahle hooks labeled as croaker or shiner hooks, while octopus hooks are also called wide-gap and live-bait hooks.

HOOKS FOR FRESHWATER BAITS

BAIT	HOOK MODEL	SIZE
CORN	BAITHOLDER	8–4
CRAYFISH	O'SHAUGHNESSY or KAHLE	6–2
CRICKETS & GRASSHOPPERS	ABERDEEN	8–4
DOUGH (POWERBAIT)	BAITHOLDER	8–4
GARDEN WORMS	BAITHOLDER	12–4
MAGGOTS & MEALWORMS	BAITHOLDER	12–8
MINNOWS & SHINERS	OCTOPUS or KAHLE	4–4/0
NIGHTCRAWLERS	BAITHOLDER	6–1
SALMON EGGS	O'SHAUGHNESSY or OCTOPUS	6–2

HOOKS FOR SALTWATER BAITS

BAIT	HOOK MODEL	SIZE
BLOODWORMS	BAITHOLDER	4–1/0
CRAB	OCTOPUS	1–3/0
CUT BAIT	O'SHAUGHNESSY	2–3/0
MULLET	OCTOPUS	1/0–4/0
PILCHARDS	OCTOPUS	1–3/0
SAND FLEAS	BAITHOLDER	12–8
SHRIMP (LIVE)	OCTOPUS or KAHLE	2–1/0
SHRIMP (DEAD)	BAITHOLDER	6–1/0
SQUID	OCTOPUS or O'SHAUGHNESSY	1–3/0

CHAPTER 4

BAIT

After choosing your tackle, sinkers and hooks, you face another very important decision: what to use for bait?

You can catch bait such as worms or minnows, make your own bait (doughballs) or buy shrimp, worms and other bait at the local tackle shop. In some cases the bait may determine the kind of fish you're likely to catch. For instance, corn works well for carp but rarely interests bass. Other baits, such as earthworms, serve as an excellent all-around option because they appeal to a wide variety of fish.

FRESHWATER BAITS

WORMS

It seems worms were created with anglers in mind. They come in different sizes, are easy to find, and they stay on the hook when casting. Best of all, nearly every kind of fish will eat a worm.

Small worms measuring from 2 to 5 inches are often called garden worms or red worms, and they make perfect bait for sunfish and stream trout. Run the hook point through the worm several times to hold it well, but leave both ends free to wiggle and attract fish. Since catfish like a bigger mouthful, put two or three garden worms on a hook to make a squirming mass that gets their attention.

Catching and Keeping Garden Worms

A few minutes of effort can produce enough bait for a day's fishing. Worms prefer rich soil, so look for them near gardens and flowerbeds. But first, check with a responsible adult to make sure it's OK to dig in a spot.

Use a shovel to turn over a clump of soil, then begin breaking it apart with your fingers to reveal any worms. If you live near a patch of woods, you can often find worms under logs or flat stones in areas where the ground is moist.

Gently catch them and put them in a plastic container (old margarine containers work well) with a few handfuls of dirt. The worms will remain in good condition until you're ready to go fishing if you put the lid on the container and keep it in a cool, dark area such as the garage or even in the refrigerator.

Nightcrawlers

Large worms measuring 6 to 10 inches are called nightcrawlers because they come out after sundown to creep through the grass. These big, juicy baits are perfect for catfish, bass and walleye. Thread a whole 'crawler

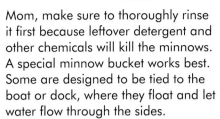

HINT BOX

Buy Fresh Bait

Just like people, fish find their food more appetizing when it is fresh. Worms should feel firm, and they should react to your touch. Minnows should swim upright in the water, not on their sides and gasping at the surface. Packaged clams, squid and shrimp should not smell foul.

Before you buy, don't feel shy! Open the container to look at or sniff the bait. Make sure it's fresh, and make every effort to keep it that way because fresh bait draws more bites.

so take slow, soft steps and use a flashlight to reveal worms stretched out on the lawn. Since nightcrawlers are very sensitive to light, a piece of red cellophane over the flashlight helps you see without alarming them. The worms come partway out of their holes but immediately disappear at any sign of danger, so you have to be quick when grabbing them. Once you have a hold, don't squeeze too tightly or pull sharply on the worm. This will break it. Gentle but firm pressure eventually causes the nightcrawler to release from its hole.

Put them in a plastic container (old margarine containers work well) with a few handfuls of dirt. Nightcrawlers will remain in good condition until you're ready to go fishing if you put the lid on the container and keep it in a cool, dark place such as the garage or refrigerator.

MINNOWS

The water's calm surface hides a fish-eat-fish world! Nearly every kind of game fish – trout, bass, walleye, pike, perch, crappie, even catfish – greedily gobbles down any other fish that will fit in its mouth.

Like worms, minnows serve as a bait that attracts a wide variety of fish. There are many different types of minnows, such as shiners, dace, chubs and killifish. The particular ones you find will depend on where you live.

You can catch minnows in special traps with funnel-shaped ends that make it easy for small fish to enter and hard for them to get out. Dry cat food is good for baiting minnow traps. You can also catch minnows with dip nets, umbrella nets and seines. Before going out to catch minnows, check your state laws to see which methods are legal, and how many minnows you may keep.

Whether you catch your own or buy minnows at the bait shop, you'll need a bucket to carry them in. If you borrow a cleaning bucket from

Mom, make sure to thoroughly rinse it first because leftover detergent and other chemicals will kill the minnows. A special minnow bucket works best. Some are designed to be tied to the boat or dock, where they float and let water flow through the sides.

Minnows must stay alive and active on the hook to attract predators, so avoid hooking them in the brain or belly. Carefully thread the hook through a minnow's lips when fishing it ahead of a split shot or on a dropper rig. When using a bobber, you can hook a minnow through the lips or in the back, just under the dorsal fin.

It usually takes a few seconds for a fish to get a minnow completely in its mouth, so don't try to set the hook as soon as you get a bite. Give the fish time to eat, and wait for it to begin swimming off before setting the hook.

SMALL FISH

Wise old anglers say, "Big fish eat big baits." While minnows work for most situations, think BIG when you're after pot-bellied largemouths, monster catfish or yard-long pike. Fishermen in Florida use 10-inch shiners as bass bait; South Carolina anglers use bream for blue cats; and anglers in the northern USA catch pike on live suckers.

You can often catch small fish on

Fact Box

WORM FARM

You can dig up a bunch of garden worms or catch a mess of nightcrawlers and keep them so you'll have a supply of bait ready whenever you want to go fishing.

An old Styrofoam or plastic cooler with several inches of potting soil makes a good "worm farm." Hot temperatures and dry soil will kill worms, so store them in a cool place like the garage or basement and sprinkle water over them occasionally. Don't drench them, add just enough water to moisten the soil.

on the hook, leaving both ends free to wiggle.

While whole nightcrawlers may be too big for sunfish to eat, they still make good bait for small fish. Cut or break the worm into short, bite-size pieces for fish such as bluegills and perch. Stream fishermen often use half a nightcrawler on the hook to tempt trout.

You can catch nightcrawlers in your own back yard. Although nearly any night will do, those after a rain are ideal. Worms can feel the vibrations you make while walking,

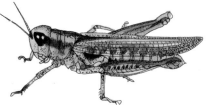

the spot and use them for bait, but make sure local laws allow this. Some states prohibit the use of game fish as bait.

Present these baits as you would minnows, hooked through the nose or back, and use heavy tackle since you're targeting larger-than-average quarry.

CRAYFISH

Resembling miniature lobsters, these freshwater crustaceans inhabit rocky-bottomed areas of streams, rivers and lakes. They are especially good baits for smallmouth bass and large trout.

Hunt for crayfish, also called crawdads, in rocky shallows. Carefully overturn flat stones and, acting quickly, try to grab crayfish before they scoot away. Crawdads use their muscular tails to propel themselves backward through the water. They look mean and nasty, but their claws can't do any serious harm. They can give you a hard pinch, though, so be careful! Some anglers break off a crawdad's claws to make the bai easier to handle.

The best way to fish a crayfish is to hook it through the tail, cast upstream and let it drift naturally with the current.

FROGS

A frog kicking across a lake's surface presents a target that bass just can't resist. For best results, hook a frog in the lips and cast it toward lily pads and weedy shorelines. Then keep it swimming back to you by slowly reeling in the line.

CRICKETS AND GRASSHOPPERS

An insect struggling at the surface sends out vibrations that attract the attention of hungry panfish, bass and trout. You can buy crickets at bait shops and pet stores (people feed crickets to their pet tarantulas and lizards).

You'll have to catch your own grasshoppers when they appear in the summer and early fall. Look for them in fields of tall grass. You'll have more success in the early morning because these jumping bugs move slowly until the sunshine warms them up.

Hook crickets and grasshoppers through the body, using light-wire Aberdeen hooks that won't weigh them down. A bobber adds necessary weight for casting.

PHOTO: CHRIS WOODWARD

MEALWORMS

Fished on small, light-wire hooks, mealworms make good bait for panfish and trout. You can buy mealworms in bait shops and pet stores.

SALMON EGGS

Available in bait shops and sporting-goods stores, salmon eggs are convenient to use and very effective for trout. Put one or two of these little round baits on a short-shank hook. In lakes, fish them under a bobber or on a dropper rig; in streams, drift them in the current. Remember to cast rather gently because salmon eggs can easily come off the hook.

DOUGH BAITS

Sporting-goods stores and tackle shops carry ready-made dough baits such as Berkley PowerBait and Eagle Claw Nitro Bait. These baits may come in different formulas designed to attract specific fish, including trout, crappie or catfish. To use them, take a small amount of dough and mold a ball around the hook.

Carp and catfish fanatics make their own doughballs, with the flavor possibilities limited only by the imagination. Creative anglers enhance their doughballs with anise, peanut butter, sardine oil, fruit flavoring and more.

HINT BOX

Do-It-Yourself Doughballs

Try this recipe for making doughballs to use as carp and catfish bait. You can also experiment with other flavors such as anise, sardine oil or grated cheese.

Ingredients:
2 cups flour
2 cups corn meal
2 cups water
2 tablespoons vanilla extract
1 package strawberry Jello

Preparation:
1. Mix flour and cornmeal in a bowl.
2. Put water in a pot, add Jello and vanilla extract, begin heating on high.
3. When water boils, slowly stir in flour and cornmeal. Let it absorb the water, then remove the pot from the heat.
4. Stir and knead the mixture until dough becomes thick enough to stay on a hook.
After it cools, put dough in a resealable plastic bag and keep it in the refrigerator until you go fishing. NOTE: The dough should be soft and pliable. If it is too dry and crumbly it will not stay on the hook.

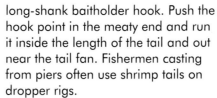

GROCERY STORE BAITS

Some fishermen get their bait at the grocery store. Trout, carp and catfish find corn appetizing. Make sure you use whole-kernel corn, and thread five or six kernels on the hook. Catfishermen take advantage of their quarry's sense of smell and tempt them with chicken liver or processed meat products like Spam.

SALTWATER BAITS
SHRIMP

Like outlaws in the Old West, shrimp are wanted dead or alive by many different fish. They make superb live bait and excellent dead bait.

Since the force exerted on long casts can fling a live shrimp off the hook, they are rarely used in surfcasting. Live shrimp work well when fishing from a boat for redfish, snook, speckled trout, sheepshead and other fish.

Run the hook point through the hard shell on a shrimp's head, right under the horn that juts out from between its eyes. Cast with a rather soft touch to avoid tearing the shrimp off the hook. This method works well when you don't have to cast very far, for example, when working a mangrove shoreline for snook and redfish.

In situations that require longer casts, like fishing shallow grass beds for speckled trout, you can hook a shrimp through the meat of the tail. This helps it stay on the hook but hampers the shrimp's natural movement a bit.

The best ways to fish a live shrimp are: weightless or with a couple split shot in mangroves and shallows; on a popping-cork rig over grass beds; or on a slip-sinker rig in deeper water.

To use a dead shrimp, break off the head and thread the tail on a long-shank baitholder hook. Push the hook point in the meaty end and run it inside the length of the tail and out near the tail fan. Fishermen casting from piers often use shrimp tails on dropper rigs.

Snook, redfish, speckled trout and flounder often fall for a jig head that has been "sweetened" with a shrimp tail.

Surfcasters targeting smaller fish peel shrimp tails and cut the meat into pieces that just cover the hook. They catch pompano and whiting this way.

BLOODWORMS

Bloodworms get the name because their pale, pinkish skin lets red body fluids show through. They burrow in sandy or silty areas and range from 2 to 12 inches or more in length. Exercise caution when handling bloodworms because they have a retractable mouth with four small teeth and can inflict painful bites.

For striped bass, use a whole bloodworm or, if they are small, put two or three on the hook. When targeting flounder or porgies, you can cut the worms into smaller pieces. A dropper rig is a good way to present bloodworms whether fishing from a boat or pier.

SQUID

Squid makes great bait because it has a powerful scent that attracts all kinds of fish, and its rather tough flesh stays firmly on the hook. Make sure you keep squid in the cooler until you're ready to bait up because it can spoil quickly in the hot sun.

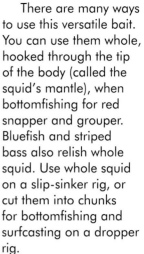

There are many ways to use this versatile bait. You can use them whole, hooked through the tip of the body (called the squid's mantle), when bottomfishing for red snapper and grouper. Bluefish and striped bass also relish whole squid. Use whole squid on a slip-sinker rig, or cut them into chunks for bottomfishing and surfcasting on a dropper rig.

Squid strips, made by cutting the mantle into lengths of 1 to 6 inches, are excellent bottomfishing and surfcasting baits. Run the hook through one end of the strip a couple times and leave the rest free to flutter attractively in the water. Squid strips also provide fantastic "tails" for jig heads.

CLAMS

They don't look like much from the outside, but open a clam and you'll see a mouthful of meat that fish (and people!) find delicious. Clams are a very popular bait for surfcasting and pier fishing because they are readily available, appeal to a wide variety of fish, and they stay on the hook during the cast.

Harvesting clams is regulated by seasons, minimum sizes and possession limits, so check state laws before gathering any for yourself. Bait shops near the shore save you a lot of trouble by selling clams. For best results, buy fresh clams in the shell and shuck them yourself. You can then put some salt on the baits and keep them in a container. As a second-best option, buy shucked and frozen clams.

Rather than baiting up with a big glob of clam guts, use only the firm meat. The meat of one clam can usually be cut into enough strips to

Live shrimp presented attractively are irresistable to many fish species

provide two or three baits. Push the hook point through one end of the strip, then run it through a couple more times to hold the bait securely on the hook. Use clams on a dropper rig.

CRABS

Small crabs, up to about 3 inches across the back, serve as good live baits for striped bass, drum and tarpon. Push the point of a short-shank live-bait hook through the edge of a crab's shell, or carapace. This will not kill the crab, so it can wiggle its legs and get a predator's attention. You won't need a sinker for casting live crabs in shallow-water situations; in deep water, use a slip-sinker rig.

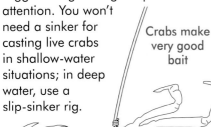

Crabs make very good bait

BAITFISH

Just about any species of small fish could be referred to as "baitfish" because larger fish see them all as potential snacks. You'll find different kinds of baitfish in different parts of the country. In the Northeast, herring are common; finger mullet are a favorite in the Southeast; and menhaden, also called pogies or bunker, occur along the entire East Coast. Common baitfish on the West Coast include anchovies and sardines.

No matter where you fish or which baitfish you have, there are several standard techniques you can use. On light-tackle in shallow water, hook the bait through the nose. You may need to add a split shot or two for better casting. When fishing over grass beds or rocky bottom, use a bobber and hook the bait in the nose or back.

In deeper water, hook baits in the nose and use no sinker if your target

Fact Box

CAST NETS

Special nets help fishermen catch a lot of baitfish in very little time. As the name implies, a cast net is "cast," or thrown, over a school of baitfish. It spreads open, and weights around its edges make it sink quickly and trap the fish. Pulling on a central hand line draws the net closed to prevent the fish from escaping.

Cast nets come in many sizes and strengths. Large, heavy cast nets are used to catch big baitfish like menhaden or blue runners. Small, light nets are good for small baitfish like sardines.

An experienced angler makes it look easy, but learning to throw a cast net takes a lot of time and practice.

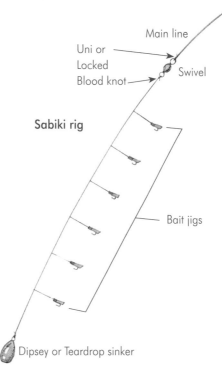

Main line
Uni or Locked Blood knot
Swivel
Sabiki rig
Bait jigs
Dipsey or Teardrop sinker

fish are swimming near the surface. Hook baitfish in the belly if you want them to swim down and away from the boat. A slip-sinker rig with the appropriately sized weight takes nose-hooked baitfish to mid depths.

For grouper and other bottomfish, use a slip-sinker rig and a rather long leader. This presents the bait in a more natural manner, especially when you hook it in the nose.

A boat's livewell has a pump to constantly renew and circulate water, thus keeping baitfish in good condition. Anglers catch baitfish with castnets or sabikis (rigs with four to 10 small hooks).

DEAD BAIT

Dead fish make good bait for grouper, snapper, bluefish, sharks and many other species. While bait shops sell frozen herring, cigar minnows and others, you should use fresh dead bait when possible.

If the baitfish range from 4 to 6 inches long, you can often use them whole on a slip-sinker rig. A good technique calls for running the hook all the way through the bait's eyes, pulling a few inches of leader through and burying the hook in the body near the tail.

Chunks of fish (called cut bait) will catch nearly anything that swims. Cut the baitfish into pieces, varying the size according to your target species. Half a baitfish may be perfect in some cases; in others you might use 1-inch chunks. Present cut bait on a dropper rig and don't forget to add

BELOW: Adding chum to the water at a pier, especially at the change of the tide, can bring the fish on to the bite.

a wire leader if sharks, bluefish or mackerel are in the area.

CHUM

What happens when you're at the movie theater and the aroma of hot

Mullet attracted by bread chum gather, waiting for the next handful.

buttered popcorn reaches your nose? You want to run over and get some popcorn, of course! You can create a similar response in fish by drawing them closer with the smell of a tempting meal.

Chumming refers to dropping bits of food (chum) in the water to attract fish and entice them to take your bait. Anglers employ this technique to target a wide variety of fish ranging from stripers to snappers to sharks. The idea is to put just enough chum in the water to get fish interested. You don't want them to fill up on chum and ignore your baited hook!

Bait shops sell "bricks" of frozen chum consisting of ground-up fish, shrimp and crabs. Fishermen put the block of chum in a mesh bag and hang it over the side of the boat. As it melts, the chum releases a steady stream of scent and little bits of food. This attracts small fish, and their activity along with the chum's smell gets the attention of larger predators. When they come closer to investigate, they find the bait.

Another method of chumming, sometimes called chunking, involves cutting baitfish into pieces and dropping them in the water. Oily fish such as menhaden or bonito work well here because they create a strong, long-lasting slick that predators can easily follow. The trick is to toss a handful of chunks out every few minutes to keep fish interested without overfeeding them. Then you put a bait chunk on an unweighted hook and let it drift back in the chum slick so a hungry fish can find it.

Position your boat up-current of structure so the chum will coax fish to come out for a look. Once you begin chumming, it's very important to keep the slick going. A good rule of thumb says toss out a handful of chunks, wait for them to sink completely out of sight, then toss out a few more. If the flow of chum gets interrupted, fish often lose interest and go elsewhere.

CHAPTER 5

LURES

Lures are artificial baits designed to attract fish. They work because they look and/or move like small fish, crustaceans or other prey that larger fish like to eat. Don't get confused by the huge number of lure styles, sizes and colors displayed at tackle shops. For starters all you need are a few lures that cast easily and resemble the sort of bait you would use for the type of fish you are after.

PHOTO: LIGIA LEITI

Selecting Lures

Casting lures is a fun and effective way to catch fish so you should always keep a few lures in your tackle box. There are many different lures to choose from, but it is best when starting out to have a selection of all-around styles and colors that will work in both salt and fresh water for a wide variety of different fish.

The thousands of lures displayed on tackle shop walls can be broken down into the following basic categories: crankbaits and minnow plugs; spoons; soft plastics; topwaters; spinners; spinnerbaits; jigs; and rattlers. Lures for saltwater species need to be a bit heavier and stronger than their freshwater counterparts, but there are many lures that work equally well in fresh water, brackish water and shallow saltwater.

For instance, traditional spoons such as the Daredevle and Johnson Silver Minnow have universal appeal and will catch many different kinds of fish in salt and fresh water. The Rapala CD Minnow is yet another classic that can be cast or trolled to catch just about anything that swims, including trout, bass and tuna. Soft-plastic lures (curly tails, shad, minnows) used on jig heads are also very versatile. They work well in fresh and salt water, shallow or deep, for sunfish, bass, redfish, snook and many other fish.

Size and Color

Every lure is not an exact replica of a baitfish. Polished metal spoons look nothing like a fish but they mimic the flash and movement of fleeing minnows that trigger predators to strike. One key to success involves using lures that closely match the size and color of naturally available food sources.

For example, a 3-inch chrome-colored spoon fools bass in lakes where gizzard shad are the main forage species. In other lakes with high populations of sunfish, a bluegill-colored crankbait will catch bass. Lures wearing wild, unnatural finishes like bright orange and chartreuse make good choices for stained or muddy water because fish can more easily see these colors.

Good anglers are observant. They notice the size, shape and color of prey species such as minnows and crayfish, and then use lures that closely imitate them.

Presentation

Where you fish, which lure you choose and whether you retrieve it along the bottom, in mid-depths or at the surface will determine the type of fish you are likely to catch.

Once you choose an appropriate lure, the next consideration is presentation (how and where you work the lure). Some anglers believe this is more important than the lure's shape and color. It is important to present lures in the "strike zone" (where fish are most likely to be feeding) because you won't catch much by just casting around aimlessly.

Saltwater fish that feed in open water, like bluefish and mackerel, might be hooked with random casting, but even these fish can be targeted more specifically. When seeking open-water fish, always look for tide lines, points or jetties that drop into deeper water or for signs of predators feeding on baitfish. This may be marked by splashes or birds feeding over a working school of fish.

Species such as bass and snook, called "ambush predators," lie in wait for their next meal close to snags, fallen trees, mangrove roots and the mouths of small creeks that join a main river or lake.

Trout tend to feed at the head and tail of a pool or along undercut banks in streams and rivers.

Knowing where and how your quarry prefers to feed makes you a better lure fisherman. Discover which forage species are available, use lures that imitate these baitfish and work them in the strike zone, and you will likely be rewarded with crashing strikes.

Speed kills

Speed is a vital ingredient in lure fishing. After casting you must retrieve the lure at a speed that is attractive to the fish. The lure's speed and action are what induce fish to strike. Fast-swimming fish like tuna and trout

need a fast retrieve, while ambush predators usually fall for a slower, more tantalizing retrieve.

Carefully watch the lure you use and check that you are retrieving it at a rate that makes it look attractive in the water.

It might seem a bit difficult at first but once you get the general idea and know how the lure should work, then things improve. You can add to many a lure's action with small, rapid twitches of the rod tip as you retriev

Trolling or casting

Lures can be presented by either trolling or casting.

Trolling is done from a boat. The angler lets out a certain amount of line – 20 to 60 feet or more, depending on the lure and area being fished – then lets the motor do the work of pulling the lure. The boat must go at a speed that keeps the lure swimming properly and in the strike zone. Trolling is very productive in lakes and large rivers for trout, bass and northern pike. It also takes saltwater fish such as tuna, king mackerel and striped bass. Clever trolling techniques can work lures around snags and other likely spots by using the boat to position the lures where fish are likely to be feeding.

Trolling covers a large area of water while casting is more selective:

the angler chooses specific targets and works the lure to draw strikes. Casting can be great fun, as you will often see the fish attacking the lure.

When casting lures you need to develop your accuracy so you can place the lure where it is most likely to be attacked by the fish. Accuracy comes with practice, so don't worry if some of the casts don't land in exactly the right spot at first. If you don't snag the lure occasionally then you're probably not putting the lure in the best place for the fish.

Crankbaits and minnow plugs

These are by far the most popular lures and come in hundreds of different shapes, sizes and actions. Different models may float, sink or suspend and, depending on the size and shape of the lip, may dive to depths of up to 30 feet. Some work best when cast and retrieved, others when trolled, and some perform equally well in both forms of presentation. Such lures include the Rapala CD, Shad Rap and Husky Jerk, and the Bomber Long A.

Small minnows and crankbaits like the Rapala CD5 and the Rebel Crawfish are terrific lures to cast for trout and smallmouth bass.

These plugs are popular because their built-in action makes them

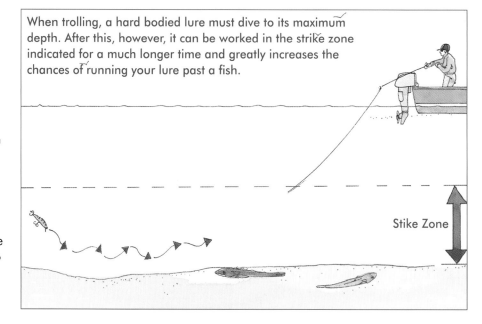

When trolling, a hard bodied lure must dive to its maximum depth. After this, however, it can be worked in the strike zone indicated for a much longer time and greatly increases the chances of running your lure past a fish.

Stike Zone

easy to use. Just cast out and reel in! The lip – the piece of plastic or metal protruding from the lure – determines action and depth. A narrow lip imparts a tight wiggle to the plug while a wide lip results in an exaggerated side-to-side motion; short lips keep lures working closer to the surface while long lips make plugs dive deep.

The retrieve or trolling speed also affects plug performance. In general, the faster you retrieve a plug the deeper it dives. But each one has its limits. Watch your lure as it moves through the water. If it swerves up and to one side, you're working it too

fast. Working a lure too slowly results in a lifeless, unattractive presentation. Try to keep a plug swimming straight ahead as the lip makes it shimmy like a real fish.

Spoons

Metal spoons have been catching fish for centuries and will continue to do so. Their flashy, wobbling action mimics a wounded baitfish and provokes predators to attack. These heavy lures cast like rockets and sink very quickly, making them an excellent option for fishing open water. They catch trout, salmon and pike in lakes, while surfcasters favor them for bluefish and stripers.

You can work spoons in two different ways. The simple approach calls for casting and letting it sink to the desired depth before beginning to retrieve at a constant rate to make the spoon wobble in a darting rhythm. The second approach often entices

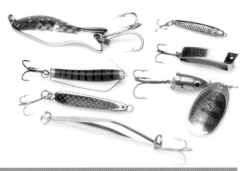

strikes from shy fish. During the retrieve, pause occasionally to let the spoon sink for a few seconds before you continue to crank the reel. Stay alert, though: Fish tend to grab the lure as it flutters down on slack line.

Some anglers dress single-hook spoons (like the Johnson Silver Minnow) with a plastic grub tail to spice up the lure's action. Metal lures will sink and snag in shallow streams, so here you should use spoons made of light plastic. Trout love them!

Topwaters

It's really exciting to see your topwater lure disappear in an explosion of water when a bass, pike, seatrout or snook hammers it. There are four types of surface lures.

Poppers such as the Arbogast Hula Popper, Rapala Skitter Pop and Storm Chug Bug are identified by their concave face, They spray water with a "pop" when twitched forward briskly with the rod tip. Most freshwater anglers pause frequently for a pop-and-stop retrieve while saltwater fish usually respond to a more aggressive presentation.

Paddlers such as the Heddon Crazy Crawler and Arbogast Jitterbug sport metal "wings" that give them action. They work best with a slow, steady retrieve and occasional pauses. Try them at night for largemouth bass.

Propeller baits have – you guessed it – small propellers that spin and gurgle as you bring the lure across the surface. Work these lures with rhythmic pulls that excite or anger fish into striking. Examples include the Heddon Torpedo and MirrOlure Prop Bait.

HINT BOX

Lure Retrieve Speed

Most freshwater anglers agree that slower retrieve speeds work best, especially when trying to keep a lure in close to the snags and other features that hold fish. However, the general rule is to retrieve your lure so it swims with its optimum action. Deep-diving plugs usually work best with a relatively slow retrieve, while small-lipped plugs and metal lures (spoons and spinners) require faster retrieves. Always watch your lure to keep it moving at an appropriate and attractive speed.

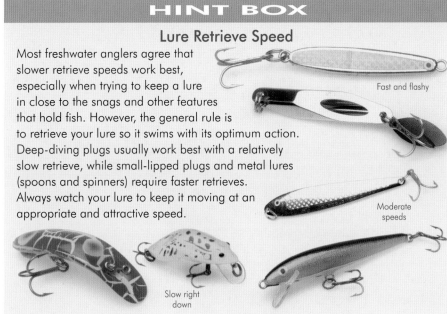

Fast and flashy

Moderate speeds

Slow right down

Walk-the-dog style lures, like the MirrOlure Top Dog and Zara Spook, move in a zigzagging pattern. It takes practice to learn to work these plugs correctly but they draw strikes from fresh- and saltwater fish alike.

If a fish strikes but misses your topwater lure, keep working it until the fish returns for another shot.

Spinners

Spinners such as Mepps and Rooster Tails are standard items in every trout fisherman's tackle box. Named for the metal blade that spins during the retrieve, these lures create vibrations that fish find attractive. Fishermen who target pike and muskellunge often use large spinners like the Mepps Giant Killer and Blue Fox Vibrax. Be sure to use a snap swivel ahead of a spinner; otherwise the lure action puts twist in the line.

Spinnerbaits

Shaped like a large safety pin with a hook on one arm and a spinner blade or two attached to the other, spinnerbaits hardly look like anything a fish would want to eat. But they have

become one of the most effective lures for largemouth bass, not to mention smallmouths, walleye and pike. Small versions of spinnerbaits, such as the Beetle Spin, prove deadly on bluegill and rock bass.

Varying the retrieve speed lets anglers use these versatile lures in many different situations. Reeling quickly makes a spinnerbait ride high in the water so you can bring it over submerged grass beds. A slow retrieve runs it deep, a perfect presentation for bass in cold weather. The spinnerbait's shape helps keep it from snagging in heavy cover.

Rattlers

Sometimes called lipless crankbaits, lures like the Rat-L-Trap and Rattlin' Rapala sink rather quickly and have a flat-faced edge that produces a super tight shake as they are retrieved. Tiny ball bearings inside a hollow chamber make these lures buzz like a rattlesnake. The noise helps predators hear the lure from afar and home in on it, even when muddy water makes it hard to see. Available in a wide range of sizes, rattlers catch everything from bass to bluefish.

Jigs

Versatile yet often overlooked, jigs consist of a hook with a weight attached. For this reason they are also called lead heads. Jig-head designs range from simple, round pieces of lead to sophisticated replicas of fish heads with holographic eyes.

Jigs dressed with hair are called bucktails and those dressed with feathers are called marabou jigs. Do-it-yourself anglers buy bare jig heads and tie on hair from squirrel and deer tails. Bare jig heads offer a quick and effective way to rig soft plastics.

You can work jigs at mid depths

with a fast retrieve or slowly hop them along the bottom.

Soft plastics

Soft-plastic lures come in many sizes and shapes. Modern molding techniques produce lifelike copies of shrimp, crayfish, salamanders and baitfish; however, simple plastic worms and grubtails still catch a lot of fish because of their enticing action. The soft, natural feel of these imitations causes fish to hold onto or attack them repeatedly until they get hooked.

As always, choose lures that imitate local forage and/or match the size of what your target fish like to eat. For largemouth bass, try plastic worms and salamanders measuring 6 to 10 inches, or plastic minnows and grubtails up to 5 inches long.

The lure's action results from the combination of its shape (many soft-plastic baits have tails that flutter or swim during the retrieve), the weight of the jig head (if rigged on one) and the way the angler works the rod tip (rapid twitches or slow upward sweeps).

The most popular way to rig soft plastics is to thread the body onto a jig head (see illustration). Jig-head presentations are easy to rig and work in a wide variety of situations for many different fish. Other methods include Texas and Carolina rigging, drop shot and wacky rigs—each of these works best for particular applications. You should use a Texas

HINT BOX

Flavored Plastic

Many anglers put a few drops of anise or fish oil with their soft plastics in a resealable bag because they feel the extra scent makes lures more appealing. Some brands of soft-plastic lures, such as Berkley PowerBait, contain scents and flavors scientifically designed to attract fish. Although they look and feel like it, Berkley Gulp! baits are not actually made of plastic. They consist of a water-soluble material that disperses a specially-formulated scent that helps fish find the lure.

PHOTO: CHRIS WOODWARD

rig in shallow water while Carolina rigs get the nod for deep water. Drop shotting should be done from a boat, and wacky rigging is the method to use when you want to just suspend a soft plastic and drift it slowly.

Many anglers now use superbraid lines when fishing with soft plastics because the thin, no-stretch lines telegraph the slightest bite back up to the rod.

Fact Box

RIGGING JIG HEADS

1. Begin by measuring the tail alongside the jig head and noting exactly where the bend of the hook comes to.

2. Turn the tail upside down and carefully push the hook point into the very center of the front or nose of the plastic.

3. Feed the plastic tail onto and around the hook bend, keeping the shank of the hook in the center of the soft plastic.

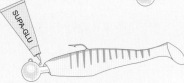

4. Bring the hook point out at the spot measured in Step 1 and as close to the centerline of the plastic as possible. Add a drop of super glue if so desired.

5. Snug the nose of the plastic hard up against the back of the jig head and check that the tail is straight and properly centered.

Fact Box

RIGGING SOFT PLASTICS

A standard **Texas Rig**. The weight may be either left free-running, or pegged in place using a sliver of toothpick or match stick pushed into the line channel of the sinker.

A standard **Carolina Rig**, with a worm hook, swivel, glass or plastic bead and running weight. The distance between the swivel and hook can be easily varied.

The **'wacky rig'** is simple and rather unsophisticated, but can be quite effective. Fish it with a gentle up-and-down jigging motion just clear of the bottom.

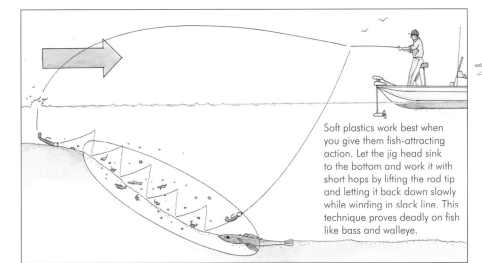

Soft plastics work best when you give them fish-attracting action. Let the jig head sink to the bottom and work it with short hops by lifting the rod tip and letting it back down slowly while winding in slack line. This technique proves deadly on fish like bass and walleye.

CHAPTER 6

WHERE TO FISH

Experienced anglers look for signs that tell them where to find fish in different situations. Learn how to read the water and you'll know the best places to cast your bait or lure, whether fishing in lakes, streams or the sea.

FOOD AND SHELTER

Two primary needs, food and shelter, have a tremendous influence on fish behavior. To put it simply: In order to survive, fish must eat and take care to avoid getting eaten.

Fish need shelter because they spend their lives dodging enemies from above and below. They have to watch out for larger fish such as bass and pike, as well as overhead danger from herons, osprey, mink and raccoons. Shelter, often called "structure" in fishing lingo, means different things to different fish. An undercut stream bank makes a good hiding place for trout, the cover of aquatic vegetation helps sunfish avoid their enemies, and bass may find protection in a fallen tree's branches.

Deep water often acts as shelter

because it gives fish a sense of security. In other cases, fish prefer deeper water for comfort's sake. For example, trout seek a lake's cooler depths as the summer sun warms water near the surface.

Darkness can also be considered a form of shelter since it helps hide fish from predators. Some types of fish feel safer and feed more aggressively at night, and as a general rule, fishing is good during low-light periods such as early morning, late evening and on cloudy days.

Fish that inhabit rivers and streams must find shelter from the current in order to save their energy. Smallmouth bass and other river dwellers station themselves in pockets of calm water behind rocks, where they don't have to fight the current to hold their position.

Since they never know when the next meal may come along, fish try

to conserve their energy when not feeding. That's why a smallmouth rests behind a rock while waiting to dart out and snatch up minnows.

Any place that offers shelter in close proximity to a food supply is likely to be a hot spot. A drop-off that lets fish rest in the security of deep water between forays to hunt baitfish in nearby shallows is very likely to hold bass.

The sudden abundance of an available food source can make fish temporarily forget caution as they take advantage of an easy meal. You can see this behavior when trout feed with abandon during a heavy mayfly hatch, or when bass attack a school of minnows at the surface.

It pays to remain observant and alert for signs that reveal the best places to find fish. The following pages offer clues as to what to look for.

FRESHWATER FISHING
Lakes

Lakes and ponds contain two basic types of structure. Visible structure, such as vegetation, is rather easily identified. It takes a bit more effort to identify invisible structure like drop-offs and ledges.

Visible Structure

Before you make your first cast upon arriving at a lake, stand on the shore and take a good look around. Instead of just flinging a bait or lure out there blindly, you can usually find specific targets and structures that are likely to hold fish.

Trees

Trees growing close to a lake's edge are potential fish magnets because they provide shade (a form of shelter) and attract insects (food). On a spring or summer day you'll often see bluegills slowly swimming just under the shady surface, waiting for beetles and ants to fall in the water. This is the perfect spot to cast a fly or redworm.

Fallen trees offer shelter to minnows and sunfish that like to hide among the submerged branches. These small fish attract bass and other large fish. As ambush predators, bass find trees to be comfortable combinations of a food source and shelter. They lurk beside or under fallen tree trunks, waiting to pounce on unsuspecting prey. A spinnerbait, crankbait or plastic worm worked carefully in and around the structure will get slammed by resident fish. It's a good idea to use heavy line (16- to 20-pound test) to avoid breakoffs when hooked fish dive for the branches.

Areas of flooded timber that contain standing, dead trees make excellent places to cast a topwater or spinnerbait because these lures don't snag so easily. Remember that fishing in heavy cover like this calls for heavy line.

Aquatic Vegetation

Ambush feeders such as bass and pickerel love to lurk under lily pads. The broad, floating pads shield the fish from overhead dangers and create shadows that help them sneak up on their victims. Water lilies have long, dangling roots that attract minnows and salamanders while frogs sit on the pads above. All this life represents a smorgasbord to a hungry fish.

The exposed treble hooks of a crankbait will become hopelessly tangled in the roots. Smart choices for fishing beds of lily pads include spinnerbaits, weedless spoons,

Likely locations for fish in lakes.

plastic worms and snag-proof frog imitations. Or try a live minnow on a fixed-bobber rig, fished close to the edge of the pads.

Aquatic plants that grow beneath the surface resemble underwater forests that host fish of all sizes, not to mention insects and amphibians. Pike, pickerel and largemouth bass are among the predators you're likely to find lurking in grass beds; smaller fish include perch, bluegill and minnows. Predators typically hide in the grass and watch for small fish to swim near.

The ideal weed bed has plants that don't rise above the surface, so you can work lures and baits just above the plant tops. Use topwaters and shallow-diving minnow plugs to draw strikes from fish hiding in the weeds. Or try this deadly tactic with a spinnerbait, plastic worm, weedless spoon or other lure that won't snag: Work the lure just above the weed tops, and pause your retrieve occasionally to let the lure sink into the weeds. Then twitch the rod tip to make the lure jump up, and continue the retrieve.

Sometimes weeds grow so thick that they form a matted carpet on

the surface. In this situation, look for small openings where you can drop a plastic worm or jig. Also, try working lures and baits as close as possible to the edge of the weeds.

Points

A point or narrow finger of land jutting out into a lake often has deeper water on either side, and fish frequently hold along the sloping bottom. Since fish usually stay near bottom here, your presentation must get down to them.

Lure fishermen can use deep-diving crankbaits or hop jigs along the bottom, while bait fishermen should try a dropper or slip-sinker rig.

Feeder Streams

A stream that empties into a lake creates several different fish-attracting situations. The influx of cooler, moving water oxygenates the immediate area and draws fish, especially in the summer months. A stream also carries minnows, insects and other food items into the lake, so fish come here to feed. They may also find shelter in the form of deeper water because feeder streams often carve channels in the lake bottom.

All these reasons make the mouth of a feeder stream an excellent place to try your luck. If the stream has a strong enough flow, a good tactic is to let a worm or minnow drift with the current out into the lake on a free line or bobber.

Docks and Bridges

Artificial structure attracts fish too! Bridges offer shade while the pilings attract minnows, so game fish often hang out under bridges. The trick is to work a bait or lure vertically beside the pilings. Try dropping a jig or spoon all the way to the bottom, jiggling it up and down for a moment, then reeling up a few feet to jiggle it again. Work it back toward the surface like this until you begin

CANOES FOR FISHING

Canoes and kayaks make very good fishing platforms in streams, rivers lakes and estuaries. They are fun to use, easy to carry and they help you to catch more fish.

Like any boat they provide mobility and greatly increase the fishing options available. You can paddle along and troll a lure, cast at snags, fish live minnows or have a drift around. The movement and stability of these craft are different than a normal boat or dinghy but you will get used to them quickly. Canoes and kayaks are fun to paddle, get you mobile, keep you fit and catch more fish. You can't beat that.

When fishing it is essential to wear a life jacket for extra safety.

catching fish at a specific depth.

Docks and boathouses offer shade and shelter along what may otherwise be a featureless shoreline. Fish swim around the legs as well as under a dock, so take the time to carefully work over every spot. Choose your offering according to the target species (for example, spoons for pike, plastic salamanders for bass, small jigs for perch or bluegill) and work it close to each dock leg. When fishing from a boat, try sidearm casts to flip lures under docks.

Fishing at the lake's edge.

Dam Walls

Manmade lakes are usually deepest near the dam, and the large, sloping wall of cement creates fish-attracting structure. Dams made of rock and rubble are even better because minnows and game fish hide in the pockets and crevices.

Exercise extreme caution and obey all warnings when approaching a dam. In many cases, people are not allowed to walk out on a dam, and boats may have to maintain a certain distance from it.

Fish often cruise back and forth along dam walls, so good methods include trolling or casting deep-diving plugs.

Invisible Structure

Some kinds of structure remain hidden from sight beneath the water. There are ways, however, for observant anglers to locate these hot spots and find good fishing.

Drop-offs

An abrupt change in depth is called a drop-off or ledge. Game fish like such spots because they feel sheltered in the deep area, yet remain close to shallow-water feeding opportunities. Some drop-offs are dramatic, where

the water may suddenly get 5 feet deeper. Others are smaller, but even a drop-off of 1 foot will hold fish.

Drop-offs may occur in areas shallow enough for you to notice the water become darker as it deepens, however, most anglers rely on the boat's depthfinder to reveal underwater structure.

Where ledges occur in depths of 10 feet or less, you can work a diving plug, jig or plastic worm on the deep side. Another good technique when fishing from a boat is to cast a jig or plug toward the shallows and retrieve the lure so it falls over the edge like a wounded baitfish.

Deeper ledges require a slightly different presentation to keep baits down in the strike zone. Troll a deep-running plug, try a Carolina-rigged plastic lure or send down a live

bait on a slip-sinker rig. Keep your offerings as close as possible to the drop-off's deep side.

Stream Beds

Manmade lakes often cover old stream beds. These channels act as long, narrow drop-offs that attract catfish, bass, walleye and other fish.

Shore-bound anglers should thoroughly work the area where a stream enters a lake. Anglers on boats can use a depthfinder to locate stream beds, but following the path of a winding stream on a lake bottom takes persistence.

Once again, the structure's depth determines the best ways to fish it. Stream beds cutting through the shallow portion of a lake can be covered by casting and retrieving lures. Deeper areas call for a vertical approach with jigs and spoons.

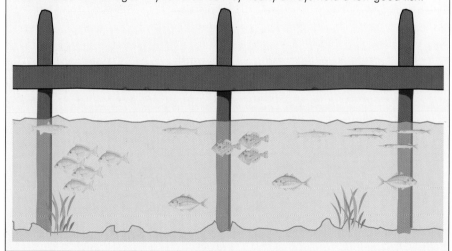

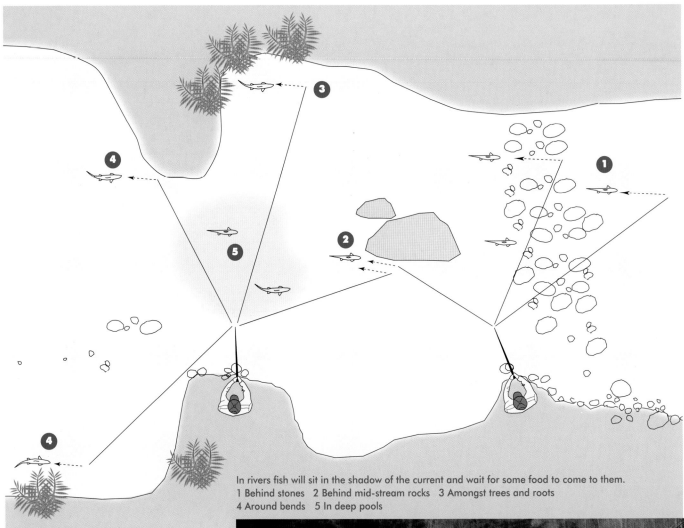

In rivers fish will sit in the shadow of the current and wait for some food to come to them.
1 Behind stones   2 Behind mid-stream rocks   3 Amongst trees and roots
4 Around bends   5 In deep pools

Bottom Types

A lake's bottom characteristics can determine which kinds of fish turn up in different spots as well as dictate the best fishing methods.

Scattered, broken rocks attract crayfish and minnows to make an area a happy hunting ground for bass and walleye. This is not the place to bounce a jig along the bottom because you'll end up losing lures to the rocks. Try suspending a jig under a slip bobber, or use floater/diver plugs. Bait fishermen should avoid sinkers in favor of bobber rigs.

A sand or gravel bottom attracts nesting bass and sunfish in the spring, and any ledges or depressions will hold game fish year round. Since there's little chance of snagging your line, you have a wide-open choice of lures and rigs.

Catfish and carp love to root

for food in areas of soft mud. Since aquatic plants tend to grow well in mud bottoms, these spots also hold bass and pike. Snags represent no problem here (unless plants grow thick), so choose the best lure or rig for your target species.

Rivers and Streams

Just as in lakes, locating fish in rivers and streams keys on finding structure.

The biggest difference involves flowing water and how fish relate to the current. Moving water acts like a conveyor belt that carries food to waiting fish, so they almost always position themselves facing into the current. It also acts like a treadmill that forces fish to expend energy in order to maintain their position.

Any creature that uses more energy than it consumes will soon

did you know ...

FISH LADDERS

Also called fish staircases, these are a series of small pools, each higher than the previous one, built beside manmade dams. They allow fish to move upstream and downstream where dams have blocked rivers. Without this movement some fish species would die out because they need to migrate so they can spawn. Trout and salmon have the ability to leap great distances up rapids, allowing them to negotiate the ladders with ease. After each upward leap they rest in the pool until ready to make the next jump.

Spinning in a mountain stream is fun and effective.

Shoreline vegetation offers fish both food and shelter.

starve, so fish in rivers must concern themselves with three important tasks: avoiding predators, finding shelter from the current, and eating. The best places to cast your line offer fish a combination of all three.

Fish are accustomed to seeing food wash downstream, so anglers should use the current for a natural presentation. Cast baits upstream of structure and let them drift past in the current for best results.

Holes and Pools

To a fisherman, "hole" refers to a deep spot in a stream. A "pool" is usually longer and wider than a hole. Both offer shelter from predators in the form of deep water, and the current tends to slow down as the water deepens, so fish expend less energy to hold their position. Best of all, any food items that tumble in with the current tend to slow down as they enter a hole, so fish can feed more easily.

Actively feeding fish usually sit at the head of a pool, where the moving water enters. They stay near the bottom and look up at the water passing overhead, ready to grab minnows or insects that wash into the pool.

Cast a worm, minnow or other bait slightly upstream of the head of the pool and let it drift in with the current. Don't cast into the middle of a pool and retrieve a bait against the current because this can spook fish that perceive it as unnatural.

A large hole or long pool could have fish stationed anywhere along its length, so make as many drifts as necessary to cover the entire area.

Spinners prove deadly on stream trout. Position yourself below a hole or pool, cast a spinner upstream and retrieve the lure so it enters with the current flow. Make sure you reel in line quickly enough to keep the spinner blade turning. This same presentation will nail river smallmouths when casting a minnow plug.

Bends

A curve or bend in a river causes water to flow faster on the outside edge and slower on the inside. Fish hold in the seam between fast and slow water, waiting to pick off minnows and other prey.

Catch trout from shore...

...or by trolling the lake.

A fishing derby at the local park.

Baiting the hook.

A steep river bank often holds fish.

Logs and other debris often pile up at a bend to create shelter where fish remain protected from predators and current while watching for food. Drift baits past these hiding places, or try "hovering" a spinner or minnow plug in the current. Stand upstream of the bend and let the lure drift down by slowly releasing line. Stop the drift when the lure gets to the logjam, and the lure will stay in front of the structure. Game fish dart out from their lair to smash the spinner or plug because it looks like a minnow struggling against the current.

Bends in streams often scoop out undercut banks that offer fish shade and shelter, so work such spots carefully.

Current Breaks

Any object large enough for a fish to hide behind serves as protection from the current. Although trout may take up residence behind a baseball-size rock, larger structures are better for attracting and holding fish.

Large stones in a river, logs laying across a stream, and other such objects obstruct the current and create a pocket of calm water. Fish stay close behind these current breaks to conserve energy

HINT BOX

Fishing on the Web

Modern fishermen use a net... the Internet! Tackle and lure manufacturers' websites contain information about their products and how to use them. You can find valuable tips to improve your fishing on these websites and many others.

LURES

*www.bluefox.com
www.culprit.com
www.doalures.com
www.luhrjensen.com
www.lurenet.com
www.mannsbait.com
www.mepps.com
www.mirrolure.com
www.purefishing.com
www.rapala.com
www.stormlures.com
www.yakimabait.com
www.yo-zuri.com*

RODS AND REELS

*www.basspro.com
www.cabelas.com
www.daiwa.com
www.okumafishing.com
www.pennreels.com
www.purefishing.com
www.quantumfishing.com
www.shakespeare-fishing.com
www.shimano.com
www.south-bend.com
www.zebco.com*

HOOKS

*www.daiichihooks.com
www.eagleclaw.com
www.gamakatsu.com
www.mustad.no
www.ownerhooks.com
www.vmchooks.com*

A lake's calm surface hides bottom structure like drop-offs and deep holes

Islands

An island stands as a big current break that forms excellent structure splitting a river or stream into two channels. As the current changes direction it often gouges deep holes near the head of an island, and this is also a good place to find logjams. Silt tends to accumulate at an island's tail end, where it may build a ledge that holds game fish. You can also find fish holding in the seam of current behind an island where the two channels reunite.

Feeder Streams

Tributaries create dynamic intersections of current while flushing food items into a river. Feeder streams deposit silt that builds up into mounds and ledges in the main river bed. It all adds up to a good place for fish to lay in wait for their next meal.

It's also worth exploring the feeder stream itself. Walleye, smallmouth and trout frequently swim upstream in search of food or spawning sites. And when the main river runs high and muddy after a rain, you can find cleaner, more fishable water in the tributaries.

Fact Box

SEEING FISH IN THE WATER

The colors and patterns that most fish wear are intended to make them difficult to see. This camouflage assures protection from predators and concealment from prey. For this reason they are hard to spot. Sunglasses with polarized lenses filter out much of the water's surface glare and make it easier to see fish.

The ability to pick out fish against their natural background is an acquired skill, and one that can be sharpened with practice. The main things to look for are movement, flash and odd or fish-like shapes. Sometimes, a certain part of the fish is more easily detected—such as its darker tail—and the rest of the fish can then be made out.

Over sand or similarly light backgrounds, the fish's shadow is often more easily noticed than its body. Classic examples of fish that can be spotted in this way include bass, trout and redfish.

Learn to scrutinize the water, not just scan it, and give every suspicious flicker, unusual shape or angular line a long, hard look.

while watching for food to come by. They dart out into the current to eat, then return to the sheltered spot.

Drift your bait very close to current breaks and let the flow carry it into the slack water so fish can find it easily. Hovering a lure beside a current break is also quite effective.

SALTWATER FISHING

The ebb and flow of tides keeps the sea in constant motion and greatly affects the behavior of saltwater fish. As rising tides cover beaches and low-lying areas, fish take the opportunity to forage in these spots while they remain accessible.

A falling tide forces fish to seek deeper water, and at the same time they feed on items flushed out by the flow.

In some areas baitfish become active on a slack tide (the period between incoming and outgoing tides, when there is little water movement), which prompts game fish to feed.

Surfcasting

At first glance a beach may seem barren and featureless but you can learn to identify spots that are most likely to hold fish. Wave action produces depressions that run parallel to the beach. Anglers call them troughs or gutters, and these valleys form between the beach and outer sand bar. They offer the perfect food-and-shelter combination to attract fish such as whiting, pompano, surfperch, drum, striped bass and bluefish.

Study the incoming waves and you'll notice they begin to break from 20 to 50 yards out. This marks the outer sand bar. The waves then settle again before breaking in the surf zone right on the beach. Troughs are located between the two lines of breaking waves.

Experienced surfcasters carry two types of outfits. A light rod with a close surfcasting rig serves for fishing the surf zone, and a heavier rod sends baits on a dropper rig farther out in the trough or beyond the sand bar. You can cast the heavy rod and leave it in a holder while you fish the surf zone with the light rod.

Pounding wave expose worms, crabs and shellfish, so whiting, pompano and perch follow and feed in the surf line as it moves with rising and falling tides. Use light tackle and clams, bloodworms or shrimp as bait to catch fish in the suds right at your feet!

A cut in the outer sand bar creates an open-ended trough that lets bluefish and bass enter, making a good place for anglers to cast topwaters and spoons for these predators. At other times it's better to zing spoons out beyond the sand bar to tempt bass, blues and mackerel.

Sometimes fish prefer a moving bait rather than one anchored in place by the sinker. It's always worth a try to cast, let the sinker settle to the bottom, wait a minute or so, then reel in a few feet. Repeat the process until you get a bite or bring the bait all the way in. You can also try a slow, steady retrieve to cover the area from sand bar to surf zone.

Fish usually feed aggressively in the surf, so if you get no bites after 15 minutes or so, move a bit farther along the beach to try a new spot.

Piers and Jetties

Fishing piers consist of elevated walkways and platforms that may extend hundreds of yards from the

This large jack crevalle was cruising just behind the breaking waves in the background.

HINT BOX

If your reel falls into the sand

Having a fishing reel fall in the sand is a common problem that all beach fishermen run into at some stage. A sand-covered reel can bring an abrupt end to a hot fishing session. Even worse, using a sand-covered reel can damage its gears.

A light covering of sand can usually be wiped or blown off without any dire consequences; however, if sand gets inside a reel. it must be disassembled for a thorough cleaning. Never wash a reel in salt water! The salt will crystalize inside the reel and cause corrosion the eat the gears.

For most reels, all you need to do is rinse well with fresh water, take the spool off and clean it, then spray lubricant on the shaft to have everything running well again.

Waiting for a bite on the jetty.

Fish find shelter among the legs of a pier.

If the pier you're visiting has a bait shop, ask the attendant about the kinds of fish in the area and the best ways to catch them. Don't feel shy about asking other fishermen for information, either.

Carry a selection of different hooks, bobbers and sinkers so you'll be ready to rig for the variety of fish encountered while on the pier.

Jetties are long, low walls, usually made of stone or cement, that act as breakwaters to protect inlets or prevent beach erosion. Like piers, they offer anglers access to deeper water and serve as fish-attracting structure. Unlike piers, jetties sit low on the water. Exercise extreme caution when on a jetty because rough seas can send waves crashing over the top.

Look for spots where the tide has carved deep holes beside jetties, and that's where you'll find game fish like stripers or snook. A jetty at an inlet may put you within casting distance of a deep channel.

Inlets and Bays

Inlets and bays contain diverse structures and depth ranges that host a tremendous variety of fish. The inlet will have a deeper channel that appeals to large fish like striped bass, snook and tarpon. Anglers catch fish in channels by drifting with the current and bouncing live baits or jigs along the bottom.

Inside the bay, tides tend to create strong current near the inlet, and fish usually feed more actively on a moving tide. Sand bars, points and rock piles give fish a place to stay out of the current while waiting to

shore, offering anglers convenient access to deep water. A pier also acts as fish-attracting structure since baitfish and other creatures that find shelter among its legs draw the interest of larger fish.

From a pier you can cast baits into the surf zone, troughs, or deep water beyond the sand bars. The exact spot and bait you choose depend on available target species as well as the individual characteristics of each pier. You might catch striped bass and bluefish from a pier in New Jersey, Spanish mackerel and pompano from one in Florida, or sand bass and salmon from a California pier.

FISH FACT

SEAHORSE

The seahorse gets its name because its head, neck and torso looks like those of a horse. It swims upright in the water swaying from side to side.

The seahorse has a versatile tail that it uses to hold itself in among seagrass and rocks, which it uses for protection and to attack its unsuspecting prey. It waits motionless until a small fish or shrimp swims innocently by and then eats it.

One of the oddest things about the seahorse is that the father gives birth to the young. The female seahorse deposits the eggs in the male's brood pouch then goes off on her happy way. When the young hatch they emerge from the fathers body and swim off on their own.

There are about fifty different seahorses world wide, ranging in size from about 25 mm to 380 mm high and they are a wide variety of colours.

Beach

Sand bar

Gutter

Cross section of a beach gutter

An incoming wave will rise and break on the sandbar where the water shallows. The force of the wave is lost so the water looks to be calm between the sandbar and the shore. But as the water pushes towards the shore, it rises again where it comes out of the gutter and into the higher level of sand.

ambush their prey. Pay attention to your presentation as the tide changes direction because fish will adjust their position to hold on the down-current side of structure.

As you move farther inside the bay and encounter shallower water, expect to find fish in holes and grass beds. Depths from 2 to 10 feet are perfect for nearly any rig or lure you choose: live baits on a free line or under a bobber, topwater lures, soft plastics, jigs or shallow-running plugs.

A rising tide floods shallow areas (called flats), allowing flounder, redfish and other species move up to feed while these spots are covered with enough water for them to swim about safely. A careful, quiet approach lets you get close to these wary fish and hook them on shrimp, spoons or jigs.

As water drains from a flat on a falling tide, fish drop into nearby channels and deep spots to await the next high tide. Locate the deepest holes in a channel and probe it with a jig, soft plastic or live bait.

Docks and Bridges

Bridges make very good fishing spots because the pilings offer game fish shelter from tidal current while they wait to pounce on baitfish attracted to the structure. Focus your efforts on the down-current side of the bridge and work baits or lures close to the pilings to tempt snook, seatrout and weakfish.

You'll often find that fish stack up behind a particular piling or in a certain spot near a bridge. There may be some feature that attracts them, such as a deep hole or ledge.

Snook, seatrout and other predators love to prowl around docks and pick off unsuspecting baitfish. Free-line a live shrimp or cast a soft-plastic lure near the legs and under docks to stir up some action.

At night, baitfish and shrimp gather around lighted docks. Game fish lurk in the nearby darkness to take advantage of an easy meal. You can hook them by casting to the shadow line created by the dock's light.

Offshore

Boarding a boat and leaving the land miles behind brings exciting possibilities of hooking large fish. Offshore angling requires heavy tackle and specialized techniques whether targeting bottomfish like grouper or cod on deep reefs, or trolling for king mackerel, tuna and sailfish.

FISH FACT

GHOST OF THE FLATS

Saltwater fly-fishermen and light-tackle enthusiasts consider the bonefish a noble adversary. Native to the warm waters of south Florida and the Bahamas, bonefish typically weigh from 3 to 10 pounds, and shiny, silver scales give them a chrome-plated appearance. Once hooked, they put up a strong fight with long, fast runs that make reel drags scream.

Bonefish prowl shallow areas, called flats, to feed on shrimp and crabs. At times the fish are in water so shallow that their tails break the surface when they lower their heads to feed. Avid anglers love to see "tailing" bonefish. Flats boats are designed to operate in shallow water, and anglers use push poles to quietly maneuver the boat within casting range of bonefish. They must approach carefully because the fish get extremely skittish and can disappear at the first hint of danger. This behavior earns bonefish the nickname Ghost of the Flats.

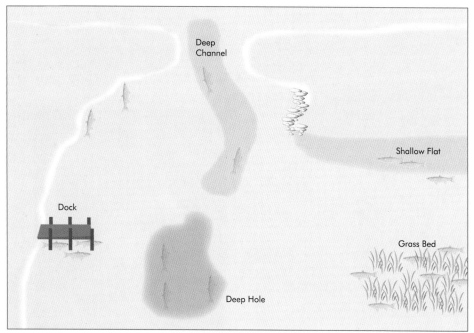

Likely locations for fish in bays and inlets.

CHAPTER 8

You've selected balanced tackle, chosen an effective bait or lure and cast to the right spot. A fish bites and you're hooked up! Now what? One of angling's essential skills involves using your tackle correctly to fight and land fish without breaking the line.

FIGHTING & LANDING A FISH

The reel's drag plays an important role in tiring fish while protecting the line. The drag is adjustable so you can set it according to your line's strength. Light lines (4-, 6- and 8-pound test) require a light drag setting. When a fish pulls hard enough, the spool turns and pays out line. This works like a safety valve to prevent the line from breaking.

Pump and wind technique

Use the rod to play a fish. Lift the rod firmly (don't jerk it) and draw the fish toward you, then wind in line as you lower the rod. Keep lifting the rod and winding down to gain line, all the time maintaining a bend in the rod.

Since slack line may let the hook fall out, apply some pressure on the fish at all times, particularly when winding down to recover more line.

Avoid dropping the rod tip too quickly because this can throw slack in the line.

Remember that reels are not winches. They store line and help play the fish but the angler has to work the rod properly to retrieve the line. When a hooked fish swims toward you, stop pumping, hold the rod up at a 45-degree angle and crank the reel quickly enough to keep a tight line. When a fish makes a strong run and pulls out line against the drag, stop reeling and hold the rod tip high.

Netting fish

After you have fought and subdued a fish, you still need to get it out of the water. More fish are lost at this stage than at any other point in the fight. The vital thing is to take your time and not rush the finish.

There are lots of ways to land

a fish. The simplest is to use the rod to lift the fish straight out of the water. This is fine for small fish, but remember a fishing line can only lift about a quarter of its breaking strain. So a 6-pound line can only lift fish of no more than 1 1/2 pounds with any safety.

To improve the odds, most anglers use a landing net. The fish is played out and then netted and safely landed. The main thing to remember with the landing net is to come from beneath the fish and lift, with the whole fish falling into the net. The person with the net holds it in the water and the angler leads the fish to the net.

Do not come from behind with the net or chase the fish around with it. Just stay calm and cool and let the angler bring the fish back to you and then take the fish correctly.

If you are on your own, you net

Netting a salmon.
1. Lead fish into the net.

2. Slide net under the fish.

3. Lift net.

4. Success!

PHOTOS: DOUG OLANDER

Once stranded, it is easy to tail grip the fish.

Play the fish to the boat and lift it to the surface. When it is in position it can be gripped firmly by the wrist of the tail and lifted aboard. The fish is then turned upside down by using your spare hand as a cradle.

The fish will feel disorientated by being upside down and will generally lay quite still while the hooks are removed. Turn the fish the right way up to release it.

Gaffing

While many big fish are released, some will be kept for the table. In locations like breakwalls and off the rocks, the only way to land a big fish is with a gaff. A gaff is a large barbless hook bound to an aluminium or fibreglass pole.

When a large fish needs to be captured, the fish is played into position and the gaff is sunk securely into the shoulder or breastplate of the fish. It is then lifted aboard or onto the rocks and the catch is secured.

Tools for releasing fish

Plastic-coated nets
Some nets have a smooth lining so the fish's protective body slime is not damaged during the landing process. Landing nets with coarse netting and knots can damage the fish's protective body slime, leading to infection in the fish following release.

The fish is still netted in the traditional manner but it can be handled safely inside the net and then released.

the fish in exactly the same way by lifting the rod to lead the fish into the net.

When fishing from the shore or beach it is possible to gently slide the fish up the bank. On a beach, big fish can be stranded by gently using the surf to surge the fish up the beach. The fish is secured by picking it up when the wave has receded.

In lakes where you have no waves to carry the fish up the shore, the best option is still a net. If you have no net you can lead the fish into very shallow water and strand it. Once stranded, gently move the fish by placing your foot (which must have a shoe on) beside the middle of the fish and then sweeping, not kicking, it up the shore.

Always be careful when landing fish you plan to release because you will want them to be in good condition.

Comfort lift

The comfort lift is an old method for gently landing fish and it works on just about all species.

The key is to play the fish out

and have it swimming on its side. The angler then places his hand, with fingers spread widely, under the balance point of the fish, usually just forward of the middle part of the fish. The fish is then smoothly lifted into the boat or onto the bank.

The fish will stay in this position for a few seconds but not for too long. Once landed, place the fish where you can handle it for releasing or keeping.

Lip Grip

You can land bass and snook by putting your thumb in the fish's mouth and lifting it by the lower lip. Be careful to avoid sticking yourself with the hook, especially when using lures with treble hooks.

Don't put your fingers in the mouths of toothy critters like walleye or bluefish! Use a net or special jaw-gripping devices, such as a BogaGrip, to handle these fish.

Tail grip

Large trout, salmon and mackerel can be easily tail-gripped and lifted aboard.

HINT BOX

Aquariums—a place to learn

Many cities have high-quality aquariums where you can observe a fascinating variety of fish.

Visiting an aquarium is great fun not just because of the fish on display, but you can learn about how fish behave in the water. Observe how different species swim and where they hold in the water column. Which fish seem restless? Which ones stay put? Try to learn things from what you see.

Some of the tanks offer great lessons in fish camouflage and how they use their colors.

If you are there at feeding time, watch how they feed. Some fish get greedy, others act shy.

A trip to the aquarium is fun but it is also a learning experience for anyone interested in fish or fishing.

Jaw grips

These grips fasten securely to the lower jaw and allow the fish to be lifted from the water, unhooked and released. They are designed to be used on larger-sized fish.

First latch onto the lower jaw and then use the grips as a handle to lift the fish while supporting its belly with your other hand. This avoids injuring a fish by putting all of the weight on its jaw when lifting.

Barbless hooks

Flattening the barb of the hook with pliers makes for the easy release of any fish. It is very popular when fishing with lures but can also be used with many forms of bait fishing.

The key here is to keep the line tight during the fight to prevent the hook from falling out.

Often the fish can be released simply by easing line pressure at the side of the boat. Otherwise, it is netted and lifted aboard and the hook or lure can be easily removed.

The other advantage of barbless hooks is they can be easily and far less painfully removed if you are unfortunate enough to get a hook in you.

CATCHING A BIG ONE

One of our sport's greatest thrills comes when you catch your first big fish. A young fisherman's first big fish often causes surprise when it gets hooked. You suddenly find yourself connected to a big one and have to make the best of it!

did you know ...

SEASICKNESS

The first time you go out on the ocean or Great Lakes is always full of excitement and expectation. As you move out of the harbor or river into open water the boat will rise and fall with the movement of the waves. At first the movement feels quite strange but you will get used to it quickly. For many first-time anglers this movement can also cause seasickness.

Seasickness happens when the fluid in your middle ear (which maintains your balance) moves about in response to the motion of the boat. This movement can confuse your body and eventually cause nausea and vomiting.

Getting seasick is not a good way to start your seagoing career.

To avoid seasickness, get a good night's sleep before you go out, eat a simple breakfast of cereal, toast, tea or coffee and take motion sickness medicine before you leave. Make sure you and your parents read the directions so you take the correct dose because motion sickness pills can cause side effects such as drowsiness.

It's easy to get excited with your first big catch.

You can improve the odds of catching that trophy if you use large lures and baits that target big fish. If you are going to try for hefty fish make sure you use gear that can handle them, it makes the job much easier.

The first thing you need to do is stay calm, cool and collected during the entire fight. Despite the excitement you need to keep a level head, do things correctly and avoid making mistakes that might cost you the fish. Try to keep a clear mind and remember exactly what happened during the fight so that you can correct or improve on it next time.

If you are fishing with your parents or friends who have caught good fish before, listen to their advice and try to follow their directions.

It is your fish, you hooked it and you can land it. But even if it ends up getting away, it was still your fish and

HINT BOX

Keeping Fish Fresh

A day on the water gives us the chance to enjoy contact with nature and, with some luck, bring home dinner. Just as you should gently handle fish you plan to release, you must also take good care of fish destined for the frying pan to ensure a tasty meal.

Handle fish with care because the delicate flesh bruises easily and gets mushy. To preserve flavor and freshness, clean fish thoroughly and put them on ice or in the refrigerator as soon as possible. Be sure to remove all innards and the gills, since these blood-rich organs can spoil rapidly.

you will benefit from the experience. Even the very best anglers lose big fish now and again.

However, your job is to focus on catching that fish and not worry about losing it. If the fish takes a lot of line let it run, do not increase the drag. Your drag should have been set correctly when you started fishing and it should still be all right. If your drag is too light, tighten it gradually with quarter turns of the drag knob. Don't take a full turn because this may be too much of an increase.

Keep good pressure on the fish and avoid giving it any slack line. Keep a bend in the rod while holding the tip high in the air, not pointed down at the water. When the fish stops running, tire it by using the pump-and-wind technique. Don't be in a hurry because rushing things can lead

to mistakes. It is much better to tire the fish while it is out away from you than to have a big, fresh fish thrashing and lunging at close quarters. That is when fish are often lost.

When the fish allows, keep pumping it back to you. Big fish often make more than one run, though the other runs are not normally as far as the first. Don't try to stop a fish cold when it powers away because this will only snap the line. When the fish finally comes close, steer it toward the net so your fishing buddy can scoop it up.

If you are fishing alone you may have to land it yourself. Just keep a cool head and tire the fish

HINT BOX

Reviving and Releasing Fish

Anglers practice catch and release for many reasons: a fish may be too small to keep; the season may be closed; releasing fish helps conserve our sport for the future.

No matter the motive, handle fish destined for release gently and carefully to avoid injuring them. The best way is to leave the fish in the water as you remove the hook, then let it swim away.

Contact with our dry skin removes a fish's protective slime. If you must pick up a fish, get your hands wet first. Even with wet hands, try to hold the fish as little as possible. And when holding a fish, avoid squeezing the belly area.

Unhook the fish and return it to the water quickly. Just think: Fish can't breathe above the surface; how long can you hold your breath under water?

Lower the fish into the water. Don't drop or throw it because smacking the surface can stun and injure a fish. If the fish is exhausted from a long fight, support it under the belly or hold it by the lip (lip grippers are great for this) while gently moving it back and forth to make water flow over the gills. You'll feel the fish gain strength until it can swim off under its own power.

a little more. It's always more fun, though, to fish with a friend or family member. Teamwork and sharing time on the water are important when landing big fish or just enjoying a day's fishing.

When that first big one comes along, stay calm and enjoy the action. You'll have a memory to cherish for the rest of your life. And don't forget to take a photos!

did you know ...

DETERMINING A FISH'S AGE

The age of a fish is determined by two methods: reading the growth rings on the scales or examining bony structures in the ears (called otoliths). In both cases, ring patterns give an accurate indication of a fish's age – just like counting growth rings on a tree stump.

Viewing scales through a low-powered microscope reveals clearly defined patterns or rings called "circuli." They can also be seen, but not easily counted, by looking through a magnifying glass.

In slow-growing fish, the rings are closer together than in fast-growing fish. In times of stress, particularly in winter when food is scarce, a definite change occurs to the scale's structure. This is known as the "winter band" and is used to calculate the age of the fish.

Determining fish ages with otoliths takes a bit of scientific know-how. The bones are carefully removed and cut into cross sections, which are then stained to highlight the rings. Although more complicated, this process results in very accurate aging of the fish.

Some ocean fish grow at astonishing rates. For example, dolphin can reach lengths of 3 feet and weights of 20 pounds in less than a year. Others, like grouper, may only grow at a rate of 1 inch per year.

Knowing how fast different types of fish grow and when they reach breeding age is very important for biologists who help decide creel limits and minimum sizes for keeping fish.

CHAPTER 9

FLY FISHING

At first glance, fly-fishing may seem complicated because of the special equipment and casting techniques. But with a bit of practice, you'll find it fun and easy to learn. Fly-fishing can add a whole new dimension to your angling enjoyment.

Aquatic insects such as mayflies, caddis flies and dragonflies make up a significant part of the diet of trout, sunfish and bass. Fish also feed on grasshoppers, ants and beetles that fall in the water. Believe it or not, tiny hooks can be adorned with feathers and hair to resemble these different bugs and fool fish into biting.

Fly tackle makes it possible for an angler to effectively cast and work these incredibly small artificials. But fly-fishing doesn't mean light tackle only. Fly-fishermen can use sizable surface poppers and minnow imitations to catch largemouths, smallmouths and pike. Saltwater fly anglers pursue striped bass, bluefish, even tuna and sailfish!

The mechanics of casting differ greatly between fly and conventional (spinning and baitcasting) tackle. With conventional gear you cast the bait or lure, and the line follows it. Since flies (whether they look like insects or not, lures used on fly tackle are called flies) are very light, they can't pull the line out. You actually cast the fly line, which then carries the fly to its destination. That's why fly lines are much thicker and heavier than regular fishing lines.

Fly Rods

While spinning and baitcasting rods look similar to each other, fly rods stand as a breed apart. The average fly rod measures 8 or 9 feet, with the reel seat at the very end of the butt. The long rod helps an angler hold the line well above the water to work it back and forth through the air when casting.

You'll notice special line guides on a fly rod. The one closest to the reel, called a stripper guide, is round and looks like those on conventional rods. The others along the rod's length are called snake guides because of their sinuous shape. The open, unrestrictive design lets thick fly line glide smoothly through the guides during casts.

Fly Reels

When casting, line flows quickly off a conventional reel. Not so with fly reels. You pull line off the reel manually, a bit at a time, and work it out the rod tip when fly-casting. And when you hook a fish, you rarely wind line directly onto the reel during the fight. Instead, you bring in the line by hand while letting the flexible rod wear down the fish.

For these reasons, fly reels are rather simple in design. They don't need fast retrieve ratios or complicated drag systems. Choose a reel that matches the rod and holds enough line for the fish you'll pursue.

Fly Line

A fly line's braided core assures strength and flexibility while an outer coating of vinyl, which varies in thickness, provides the weight and shape necessary for casting. The coating's configuration determines the line's taper, which in turn has a great influence on how it behaves during the cast.

As the name suggests, a level taper has the same thickness from end to end. A double taper has a uniform middle section and gets thinner at each end. These two tapers can be difficult for beginners to cast. New fly-fishermen should use a weight-forward taper, which is easier to cast because the front end is thicker and heavier than the rest of the line.

Anglers must choose a floating or sinking line according to which flies they will use and where. Casting dry flies or poppers calls for floating lines, which also work for fishing nymphs and streamers in shallow water. Probing the depths with streamers requires sinking lines, but they are rather heavy and awkward to cast. A sink-tip line (only the forward end sinks) makes a good compromise for fishing nymphs and streamers in mid depths and proves a bit easier to cast.

Backing

When spooling up a fly reel you must first put on 50 to 100 yards of Dacron or braided line as backing. Since fly lines measure 100 feet or less, you'll need the extra line if you hook a large fish that makes a long run. The backing also fills the spool and makes it easier to retrieve the fly line.

Leader

Since fish can easily detect a thick fly line, anglers must use monofilament leaders to avoid spooking their quarry. Leaders also get gradually thinner toward the tip, which helps transfer energy from the fly line for smooth casts.

A tapered leader (don't confuse it with the fly line's taper!) begins with a butt section of heavy monofilament, about 50-pound test, which attaches to the fly line. Two or three short lengths of mono follow, each thinner than the previous section. The last and lightest segment of the leader is called the tippet; the fly attaches here.

Casting dry flies to wary trout demands leaders of 12 feet or longer. You can use a much shorter leader for bass and panfish.

You can buy ready-made tapered leaders or construct your own by joining segments of monofilament with double-uni knots.

Arbor Knot (backing to reel)

Knots from reel to fly

Albright Knot (backing to fly line)

Nail Knot (fly line to leader butt)

Double Uni Knot (tapered leader section)

Clinch Knot (tippet to fly)

Double Uni Knot (leader to tippet)

How to tie a Nail Knot

1.
Leader Butt
Line
Small tube or nail

2. Hold the leader and tube against the fly line. Working back towards the leader's standing end, wrap the tag eight times around the tube, fly line and leader.

3. Run the tag end through the tube (or alongside the nail), taking care to hold the wraps tight. Pull the tag and tube out slowly and carefully while tightening the wraps. Don't let the wraps overlap each other.

4. Hold the tag end with pliers and cinch the knot. Trim the tag.

HINT BOX

BASIC FLY SELECTIONS

Fly patterns come in a mind-boggling variety that may leave beginners feeling dizzy. You don't need a vast and sophisticated collection to enter the fun world of fly-fishing. The following assortments will get you started. As you gain experience you can add flies that work well in your particular area.

THE FLIES

NYMPHS
Nymphs represent an aquatic stage in the life cycle of insects such as mayflies and dragonflies. They come in many different sizes and colors, and are a very common food item for fish. A good way to fish them is to drift the fly in the current near the bottom in rocky areas of streams and rivers.

WET FLIES
Called "wet" because they are meant to be fished beneath the surface, these flies imitate a variety of bugs from drowned bees to caddis fly pupae. In streams, drift them through spots likely to hold trout. In lakes, sunfish can't resist a wet fly retrieved slowly with frequent pauses.

DRY FLIES
Mayflies, caddis flies and other insects spend part of their lives in the water, then transform into winged adults. Before taking first flight they float on the water, and they later return to lay eggs at the surface. Dry flies imitate these delicate creatures that fish find so tasty. Because trout give away their position when picking insects off the surface, anglers can often "sight-fish" to individuals. They must make accurate casts so the dry fly drifts naturally over the fish.

STREAMERS
Not all flies imitate insects. Streamers resemble minnows and make a good choice for targeting fish with big appetites such as largemouth and smallmouth bass and hefty trout. The "down and across" presentation works well with streamers. Cast across the flow in a slightly down-stream direction and let the current sweep the fly past fishy-looking spots like rocks and logs. In lakes, make long casts and let the streamer sink for several seconds. Then retrieve it by "stripping" the line, which means taking short pulls to make the streamer jump forward then sink during slight pauses.

POPPERS
Made of cork or plastic, poppers float high on the surface and have a flat or concave face. Tug the line sharply and they make a loud noise that attracts bass and panfish. While pausing for long minutes between pops, give the line gentle tugs to make the popper quiver and send out tiny waves. This trick goads fish into attacking.

THE SELECTIONS

BASS (LARGEMOUTH and SMALLMOUTH)
Surface Flies
• Deer-hair bugs (sizes 1, 2) • Foam poppers (sizes 4, 6, 8)
Streamers
• Black Marabou streamers (sizes 4, 6, 8) • White Marabou streamers (sizes 4, 6, 8) • Muddler Minnows (sizes 4, 6, 8)
Nymphs
• Dragonfly nymphs (sizes 6, 8)
• Woolly Buggers (various colors, sizes 4, 6, 8)

TROUT
Dry Flies
• Adams (sizes 10, 14, 18) • Black Gnat (sizes 10, 14, 16)
• Blue Wing Olive (sizes 12, 16)
Nymphs
• Hare's Ear (sizes 8, 12, 16) • Pheasant Tail (sizes 12, 14, 16) • Woolly Worm (sizes 4, 6, 10) • Zug Bug (sizes 8, 10,12)
Streamers
• Mickey Finn (sizes 6, 8, 10) • Muddler Minnows (sizes 6, 8, 10) • White Marabou streamers (sizes 6, 8, 10)

PANFISH
Surface flies
• Black Gnat (sizes 10, 12) • Panfish poppers (sizes 8, 10)
• Royal Coachman (sizes 10, 12)
Nymphs
• Hare's Ear (sizes 10, 12) • Woolly Worm (sizes 10, 12)
Streamers
• White and Black Marabou streamers (sizes 8, 10)

CHAPTER 10

WEATHER

Weather conditions can have a big effect on what you catch as well as your personal comfort.

Because most of us go fishing for fun, the best days are always those with clear skies and light winds. However, fish live in a very different world from ours. There is no rain or wind beneath the surface, yet fish still seem to be affected by the weather.

The reasons for this are not well known but bad weather, particularly strong wind, usually means poor fishing. Days with heavy cloud cover and perhaps a little rain but not much wind are often very good for fishing. Clouds block the sun, and fish tend to remain active and feed more during low light levels.

Other things that can influence fish include a rapidly falling barometer, which will usually put fish off the bite.

Bright, calm days with clear water can also make fish very wary. They are worried about predators and very cautious about biting in such conditions.

Strong winds make most types of fishing difficult. The only advantage may be longer casts if the wind is blowing from behind you. The problem with strong wind is that it disrupts your usual fishing style. It's hard to use bobbers or set out bottomfishing rigs and often the fish just don't bite very well on windy days.

Weather is an important part of your day's fishing so always pay attention to the forecast. Keep a log of the weather conditions when you do catch fish. You can use this information to catch more fish in the future.

Time and tide

Fish can be caught at any time of the day but they often bite best early in the morning and late in the afternoon. This is because these times allow the fish better feeding opportunities with low light levels, which help protect them from predators.

However, some fish are available at most times throughout the day and a little experience and careful observation of other anglers will soon tell you what is around and when.

If fishing in saltwater you should always be aware of what the tide is doing because it has an important bearing on your fishing. Even simple things like which side of the wharf you should fish on will be determined by the tide's movement. You always fish on the side of the boat or wharf that has the current carrying your line away from you. Fishing the other way would carry your line under the boat or wharf and make fishing very difficult.

Tidal movements have a very strong influence on the feeding habits of many fish.

A rising tide, for instance, allows fish access to feeding areas like sand flats, weed beds and mangroves; a falling tide forces them back into the channels as water drains from the shallows. Predatory fish that feed on smaller fish are more likely to be active on a falling tide as the small fish, shrimps and crabs are forced back into the channels by the tide. The time of still water between tides is always a prime feeding time for most fish. The lack of tide allows them easy movement to search for food.

Tidal forces affect each area differently as well. Tides tend not to have very much effect in a big harbour or bay, but they have a great influence in coastal rivers and the channels that feed lakes and bays.

The important thing is to know what the tide is doing during your fishing day. If you get results when the tide is at a particular stage, try to match that tide the next time you fish in the same place.

Personal protection

Fishermen need protection from the weather and the elements. All anglers need SPF 30+ sun protection

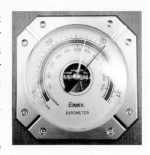

Fact Box

BAROMETERS

A barometer is an instrument for measuring atmospheric pressure, which is the basis of all accurate weather forecasting. A barometer reading of 1016 millibars represents normal air pressure. Meteorologists consider a reading below this to be low pressure and a reading above it as high pressure.

In general, decreasing atmospheric pressure (a "falling" barometer) indicates bad weather moving into the area. Increasing pressure (a "rising" barometer) signals stable weather and clear skies are on the way.

Many species of fish are responsive to changes in atmospheric pressure, often feeding actively as the barometer falls immediately before a spell of bad weather. Trout are much affected by atmospheric pressure. When the barometer begins to rise, so do the trout.

whenever they go out. Sunburn is bad news, so wear sun-safe clothing like a long-sleeve cotton shirt and a hat.

The wind and spray can also make you very cold so a windbreaker or light rain jacket is a handy thing to carry. They weigh next to nothing and

can fit into a very small space in your bag, and you'll feel glad to have one when you need it.

Always remember to dress for the expected weather conditions. If it is going to be cold then dress in layers. You can always take off a layer of clothing if it gets hot.

A rolling storm front heads across an estuary. These fronts often have dangerous winds and heavy rain.

CHAPTER 11

ETHICS ENVIRONMENT & SAFETY

Fishing is a very enjoyable pastime that puts us in direct contact with nature. The aim of going fishing is to have fun and to catch fish that are good to eat.

ETHICS & ENVIRONMENT

Everyone who goes fishing has a duty to care for the environment. Without clean water and a healthy environment we will have no fish. As an angler you are using a natural resource and you have a responsibility both to the fish and the environment. It is important to keep only the fish you want for food and bait. All unwanted fish should be returned to the water safely.

Some fish like saltwater catfish and stingrays are considered as pests. Anglers sometimes kill these unwanted fish so they can remove their fish hooks. These fish, like all others, have an important role to play in the ecosystem. Since you can get injured trying to handle catfish and stingrays, the simple answer is to just cut the line close to the fish's mouth and release it—hooks are cheap.

Anglers inevitably catch small, unwanted species and undersized fish as part of a normal day. You should respect these fish and let them go unharmed.

If you enjoy the aquatic environment you also have a responsibility to care for it. Don't throw any litter into the water. If you buy bait in plastic packets, make sure you either take the packets home for disposal or put them in the nearest litter basket.

If you want to be a real angler you need to care for the fish and the water they live in.

SAFETY

Fishing may not present the same risk of injury as contact sports like football, karate or even mountain biking, but avid anglers still get their share of cuts, bumps and bruises. Every year you hear of fishermen who fall out of boats or get carried off by rain-swollen rivers to their deaths. Taking a reasonable amount of care can virtually eliminate the chance of serious injury but, unfortunately, it is impossible to avoid all accidents. You will probably suffer some sort of injury at some time while fishing. Luckily, the majority of these are minor. As most of us learn by our mistakes, we tend not to repeat things that hurt us once we've been cut, stung or whatever. With experience you will have fewer accidents; here we are attempting to prevent or to reduce the effect of those early accidents.

It always helps if you learn some of your fishing skills from more experienced anglers. They can also show you any dangers and how to avoid them. However, in the end you are responsible for yourself.

Anywhere we fish can hold potential dangers. Jetties, docks and piers have many obstructions and tripping hazards. The pylons are often covered by barnacles that can inflict nasty cuts. Falling or being thrown from a boat is a constant possibility. The banks and edges of lakes and rivers are often steep and undercut, while the apparently firm bed of a lake or river often has soft mud covering deep holes. The temperature of the water, especially in the northern states and early in the season, is often very cold and can seriously affect your ability to swim if you suddenly find yourself immersed in it.

All boats must have life jackets—correctly known as personal flotation devices or PFDs—for every passenger on board. We recommend that you wear one at all times when in a boat regardless of the law. If you

Safety first! Wear a PFD when in a boat.

are using an inflatable PFD, make sure you know how to inflate it in an emergency.

Finally, you cannot control the actions of other anglers around you. Be aware of what they are doing and whether it poses any risk to you. If necessary move away from them—your safety is more important than any fishing spot.

Here are some hints to help you have a safe and enjoyable fishing trip:

- Always fish with a friend or two. This is especially important when fishing in remote areas where you can become lost and in areas where the water is "active" (rivers, the beach or from a boat).
- Take care around obvious hazards like rocks, cliffs, slippery or undercut river and lake banks and boat ramps.
- Take care when fishing around areas that have a lot of activity, like jetties or boat ramps, and at the start and end of a fishing trip when you may be excited or tired.
- Learn and follow the safety rules when in a boat or canoe.
- Keep the area within a boat clear to avoid tripping or falling.
- Learn where the safety equipment in a boat is kept and how to use it.
- Knives and hooks are sharp. Learn to use them safely and store them where they can't hurt anyone when they are not in use.
- Learn how to recognize and handle dangerous fish. Remember that most fish are dangerous if handled incorrectly.
- Never take risks with things you don't know or understand. When in doubt ask for help.

OXYGEN

Oxygen is the gas our lungs extract from the air we breathe. It keeps us and all other animals alive. While mammals extract vital oxygen through their lungs, fish extract oxygen from the water using their gills. Dissolved oxygen is present in water and it is just as essential to fish as it is to mammals. Dissolved oxygen levels in water are governed by a range of factors including water movement and temperature.

Algae and aquatic plants also turn carbon dioxide into oxygen through photosynthesis during daylight hours, just as land plants do. This oxygen is also released into the water. Some areas always have high oxygen levels in the water. Surf zones, pools below waterfalls and fast running water always hold more oxygen than still water. Cold water is always better oxygenated than warm water, and running water better oxygenated than still.

Different fish need different levels of oxygen. Fast-swimming species like trout need more oxygen than slow-moving species such as carp and catfish.

- Be prepared to ask for help from more experienced fishermen. Most anglers are friendly and are always ready to help someone who is willing to learn.
- Take your time! Many accidents happen because people rush when a more steady, deliberate approach is needed.
- If you are fishing with an experienced angler or boater, follow their suggestions and advice. With their experience they will know how to avoid problems.

Use your head, keep your eyes open and avoid accidents—it's important for you and your friends.